Pocket
ABU DHABI

TOP SIGHTS · LOCAL LIFE · MADE EASY

D1506789

Jenny Walker

In This Book

QuickStart Guide

Your keys to understanding the city – we help you decide what to do and how to do it

Need to Know
Tips for a smooth trip

Neighbourhoods
What's where

Explore Abu Dhabi

The best things to see and do, neighbourhood by neighbourhood

Top Sights
Make the most of your visit

Local Life
The insider's city

The Best of Abu Dhabi

The city's highlights in handy lists to help you plan

Best Walks
See the city on foot

Abu Dhabi's Best...
The best experiences

Survival Guide

Tips and tricks for a seamless, hassle-free city experience

Getting Around
Travel like a local

Essential Information
Including where to stay

Our selection of the city's best places to eat, drink and experience:

⊙ **Sights**

✖ **Eating**

🅰 **Drinking**

✪ **Entertainment**

🅐 **Shopping**

These symbols give you the vital information for each listing:

☏ Telephone Numbers	✚ Family-Friendly
⊙ Opening Hours	🐾 Pet-Friendly
🅿 Parking	🚌 Bus
🚭 Nonsmoking	🚢 Ferry
@ Internet Access	Ⓢ Subway
🛜 Wi-Fi Access	🚋 Tram
☑ Vegetarian Selection	🚆 Train
🖹 English-Language Menu	

Find each listing quickly on maps for each neighbourhood:

Bar Hemingway

16 🅰 Map p233, B2

Legend has it that Hemi
self, wielding a machine
...erate this timber-pan
...ered bar during
...showpiece is a
...en by Papa ar
...town. Dress
...s.com; Hôtel Rit
...; ⊙6.30pm-2a

Lonely Planet's Abu Dhabi

Lonely Planet Pocket Guides are designed to get you straight to the heart of the city.

Inside you'll find all the must-see sights, plus tips to make your visit to each one really memorable. We've split the city into easy-to-navigate neighbourhoods and provided clear maps so you'll find your way around with ease. Our expert authors have searched out the best of the city: walks, food, nightlife and shopping, to name a few. Because you want to explore, our 'Local Life' pages will take you to some of the most exciting areas to experience the real Abu Dhabi.

And of course you'll find all the practical tips you need for a smooth trip: itineraries for short visits, how to get around, and how much to tip the guy who serves you a drink at the end of a long day's exploration.

It's your guarantee of a really great experience.

Our Promise

You can trust our travel infor-mation because Lonely Planet authors visit the places we write about, each and every edition. We never accept freebies for positive coverage, so you can rely on us to tell it like it is.

The Best of Abu Dhabi 123

Abu Dhabi's Best Walks

Abu Dhabi's Best...

Survival Guide 143

Quick Start Guide

Welcome to Abu Dhabi

The largest hand-loomed carpet, the fastest roller-coaster, the highest high tea, the tower with the greatest lean, the largest cluster of cultural buildings of the 21st century – Abu Dhabi is not afraid to challenge world records. Welcome to an exciting city where nothing stands still...except, perhaps, a heron in the capital's protected mangroves.

Abu Dhabi cityscape
ALLAN BAXTER/GETTY IMAGES ©

Abu Dhabi
Top Sights

Sheikh Zayed Grand Mosque (p90)

One of Arabia's most magnificent mosques and a symbol of welcome to the city, it's open to non-Muslims.

Emirates Palace (p40)

You know you're somewhere uniquely Gulf when the burger is made of camel, the coffee is scattered with gold leaf and the ATM dispenses ingots.

MATTEO COLOMBO/GETTY IMAGES ©

JOCHEN TACK/GETTY IMAGES ©

Abu Dhabi Heritage Village (p42)

Watch Emirati visitors enjoy the Bedouin part of the village and Abu Dhabi's heritage is quickly revealed. Dhows passing the towering skyline opposite highlight the city's rapid pace of change.

Abu Dhabi Corniche (p24)

Reclaimed from the sea, planted with scented trees and made accessible through walking and cycling paths, the Corniche and its public beaches are the jewel in the crown of this green capital.

Manarat Al Saadiyat
(p76)

Few modern cities can match the cultural ambitions of Abu Dhabi, which claims the only branch of the Louvre outside France. This exhibition explores the planned cultural district and the inspiration behind the award-winning architecture.

Yas Marina Circuit
(p104)

Home of the Abu Dhabi Grand Prix, set beside the spectacular Yas Viceroy hotel and marina, the circuit offers year-round activities. The ride at nearby Ferrari World gives the Formula One cars a run for their money.

Abu Dhabi Falcon Hospital (p118)

Falcons occupy a special place in the heart of Emiratis, as witnessed in the waiting rooms of this specialist clinic. Tours help visitors understand the close bond between bird and owner.

Arabian Saluki Centre (p120)

Shaggy-eared or smooth-tailed, fast-paced salukis have been the Bedouin's best friends for centuries. This breeding and training centre allows visitors to come nose to nose with the affectionate hounds and their puppies.

Sowwah Square (p64)

With some of the most exciting buildings in the newest part of town, this square is the focus of developments on Al Maryah Island. The Galleria adds glamour to the city's new business district.

Masdar City (p106)

Built as an experimental project to explore environmentally sustainable urbanisation, Masdar City is powered by solar energy and encompasses a host of other green features. A self-guided tour leads around the key sights.

Abu Dhabi
Local Life

Insider tips to help you find the real city

There's pleasure in rooting out the city's heritage, browsing old souqs and exploring mangrove forests. Overlook Abu Dhabi's modern core, however, and you'll miss the point. The city has embraced the 21st century and invites visitors to do the same.

A Walk in the Park (p26)

▶ City life
▶ Cafes

In a city of 50°C temperatures, life is often lived in air-conditioned interiors. Town planners, however, have provided many opportunities to stray outdoors. Grab a hat and see how residents connect with the earth in a city of concrete and steel.

Markets of Al Mina (p78)

▶ Tradition
▶ Shopping

The mania for malls in Abu Dhabi is regionally shared, and for good reason. Collecting items for trade, which are organised by kind, sheltered under one roof and accessible on foot, is an ancient practice. Browse Al Mina's markets and the mall's origin becomes apparent.

A Nation of Seafarers (p44)

▶ Beaches
▶ Sea views

To understand Abu Dhabi's psyche, you have to engage with the water. Pearls once powered the economy and respect for the sea remains deeply engrained. Ride a dhow, eat fish, enjoy sundowners on a catamaran and see how the coast defines the capital.

The Gentler Side of Yas (p108)

▶ Watersports
▶ Nature

Yas Island is the place to go for high-octane motoring excitement, but surprisingly there's a more measured pace to be enjoyed as well. Think cycling and and kayaking, or better still, don't think at all as you paddle off into the cloudless sunset.

Gold jewellery for sale

The beach at Abu Dhabi Corniche (p24)

Other great ways to experience the city like a local:

Corniche Beach (p24)

Abu Dhabi Pearl Journey (p96)

Café Arabia (p98)

Qasr Al Hosn Festival (p30)

Du Forum (p117)

Women's Handicraft Centre (p86)

Grand Stores (p73)

Saudi Cuisine VIP (p54)

Centre of Original Iranian Carpets (p58)

Abu Dhabi
Day Planner

Day One

☀ Begin this citywide tour of Abu Dhabi at the magnificent **Sheikh Zayed Grand Mosque** (p90; closed Friday morning). Board the **Big Bus** (p50) here and enjoy the drive beside the Eastern Corniche mangroves. Alight at **Abu Dhabi Mall** (p72) and explore the **Khalifa Centre's** (p73) regional craft shops opposite. Continue on the Big Bus to **Manarat Al Saadiyat** (p76) to learn about the city's feisty future, built on a pearling past – a past encountered at nearby Al Mina's **dhow harbour** (p81).

☀ Have lunch at harbourside **Al-Arish** (p126), serving lavish Emirati buffets. Visit the neighbouring fish market then hire a bike from **Funride** (p68) opposite the Sheraton and cycle part of the 8km to the public beach, enjoying the city's impressive skyscrapers en route. Ascend **Jumeirah's Etihad Tower** (p55) for the highest high tea in Abu Dhabi.

☾ Dine on a signature camel burger at **Le Café** (p54) in the opulent **Emirates Palace** (p40) and enjoy post-dinner drinks in glamorous **Etoiles** (p55), before rejoining the real world with coffee and *sheesha* at one of the late-night Breakwater cafes.

Day Two

☀ Set the scene for today's exploration of the city's roots at the **Heritage Village** (p42) with its traditional architecture, local crafts and photographs of city founders. Stand under the giant **Emirati flag** (p48) and admire the achievement of the Nahyan family in building a great capital on little but sand. Get closer to the founding father at the **Sheikh Zayed Centre** (p48), housing memorabilia in fine traditional buildings. Delve into the city's heart along Zayed the First St, pausing to explore Khalidiyah shops showcasing local arts and crafts.

☀ For lunch, choose a backstreet favourite like **Lebanese Flower** (p32) from among many regional kebab shops then walk east past **Qasr Al Hosn** (p30), the oldest building in town. Pass the **street sculpture** (p30), symbols of core Arab values, to reach the **Central Market** (p37), site of the city's original souq.

☾ Walk along busy Hamdan St and admire the city's evening lights before turning south to the **Gold Centre** (p36); the jewellery here features pearls, upon which the city's pre-oil economy was founded. Dine at **Al Ibrahimi** (p33) opposite for a flavour of local life.

Short on time?
We've arranged Abu Dhabi's must-sees into these day-by-day itineraries to make sure you see the very best of the city in the time you have available.

Day Three

☼ If the first two days were all about seeing, this day is all about doing. Yas Island is Abu Dhabi's activities hub and what better way to arrive than by **seaplane** (p113). Stay in the fast lane in a behind-the-scenes tour of **Yas Marina Circuit** (p104), or better still get behind the wheel in a driving experience at Yas Central.

☀ Rev up for a lunch of somersaults in **Rogo's** (p115), where the burgers are delivered by rollercoaster. If you have the stomach for it, ride the real thing at neighbouring **Ferrari World** (p111), offering the fastest ride in the world. Continue the adrenalin rush at **Yas Waterworld** (p112) on 43 Arab-themed rides, slides and liquid entertainments, in search of a lost pearl.

☾ With resources depleted, fuel up at one of the Viceroy's buzzing restaurants, followed by after-dinner drinks at pit-stop **Iris** (p115) with a view of the Viceroy's spectacular lasers and lights. Grab a graffiti-clad limo and pump it up at manic **O1NE** (p117), an eccentric nightclub with 3D projections.

Day Four

☼ Slow down the pace today for a gentler engagement with the city and its nonhuman inhabitants. Begin by visiting the **Falcon Hospital** (p119) and watch a raptor flying display. Call in for a cuddle at the neighbouring **Saluki hound pound** (p121), kennels for the favoured dogs of the Bedouin. Spare 90 minutes to complete the tour of nearby **Masdar City** (p106), a pioneering concept in environmentally sustainable living.

☀ Eat a healthy lunch at Masdar's **Organic Foods & Café** (p107) then head for a relaxing afternoon on sociable **Yas Beach** (p109). When the heat wanes, join a **kayak ecotour** (p109) through the mangroves to explore this remarkable habitat, rich in bird life. Take the free Yas Express to Saadiyat Island, spotting gazelle and dolphins en route. The Saadiyat **beach clubs** (p84) offer detoxing sundowners and a dip in the sea as the sun sets – you may see a turtle awaiting nightfall to come ashore to nest.

☾ Revitalise in the spa, then prepare for supper on the outside terrace of **Turquoiz** (p86), a perfect venue for a lightly grilled catch of the day.

Need to Know

**For more information,
see Survival Guide (p143)**

Currency
United Arab Emirates (UAE) dirhams (Dh)

Language
Arabic, English

Visas
Free 30-day visas available on arrival for 34 nationalities, including most Western nationals.

Money
ATMs widely available. Credit cards accepted in most hotels, restaurants and shops.

Mobile Phones
Mobile phones operate on GSM900/1800. Local SIM cards cost from Dh55 and include Dh5 free credit. 3G is widely available, 4G increasingly so.

Time
GMT plus four hours.

Plugs & Adaptors
Electrical current 220V. British-style three-pin wall sockets are standard. North American visitors require an adapter and a transformer.

Tipping
Not generally expected in restaurants and taxis. Service charges are added to restaurant bills. Tip porters around Dh2.

① Before You Go

Your Daily Budget

Budget less than Dh600
► Budget hotel room Dh250–450
► Excellent cheap local eats (shwarma, vegetable curries, mezze)
► Free sights and public beaches

Midrange Dh600–1400
► Double room Dh500–750
► Two-course dinner Dh150–450, plus wine

Top end over Dh1400
► Five-star room from Dh1000
► Fine dining from Dh500, plus wine

Useful Websites

Lonely Planet (www.lonelyplanet.com/united-arab-emirates/abu-dhabi) Destination information, hotel bookings, traveller forum and more.

Visit Abu Dhabi (www.visitabudhabi.ae) Excellent official visitor website for travel planning and tourism.

Culture in Abu Dhabi (www.cultureinabudhabi.ae) Useful website with information on events, arts and sights.

Advance Planning

Three months before Check visa regulations, especially if combining a visit with Oman. Book tickets and hotels (Yas Island) for the Grand Prix. Check expected temperature for challenging heat.

One month before Make reservations for top restaurants.

One week before Book various activities and 4WD car hire.

48 hours before Book 2WD car hire (high season).

② Arriving in Abu Dhabi

As befitting the capital of the Emirates, infrastructure in and around Abu Dhabi is excellent and arriving in the city presents no special difficulties. Highways are well signposted and well maintained.

✈ From Abu Dhabi International Airport

An airport shuttle bus (Dh4) links the airport with Al Zahiyah, stopping at the main bus terminal en route. Reasonably priced, metered taxis are available for Yas Island and to all points of the city. Some four- and five-star hotels operate free shuttle buses from the airport. Car hire desks are available in the arrivals hall.

🚌 From Dubai

Buses to Abu Dhabi leave from Dubai's Al Ghubaiba station every 40 minutes (singles Dh20, return Dh40) between 6am and 11pm. The trip takes about two hours. Alternatively, driving yourself takes the same amount of time.

✈ At the Airport

For two decades or more, the arrivals hall at Abu Dhabi International Airport, with its tiled mushroom-shaped dome, was one of the ways in which travellers knew immediately that they had landed in the Middle East. The tradition of providing more than just a transport experience continues today with lots of shopping (including duty free) and dining opportunities in the newer part of the airport, tourist information, meet and greet services, banks and ATMs, and many car rental agencies.

③ Getting Around

Getting around Abu Dhabi's main points of interest is easy. Most visitors use taxis as they are frequent, metered, usually clean and relatively inexpensive. Navigation is mostly by landmark or Satnav (GPS), not by street name, so come prepared. There is also a very good bus system.

🚌 Public Bus

There's an excellent, air-conditioned bus network that travels along set routes throughout the day and night. Download a map from the Abu Dhabi Bus Services (dot.abudhabi.ae) website.

🚌 Big Bus Tour

Linking all the major sites in the city and connecting with Yas Island, the double-decker, air-conditioned Big Bus provides a convenient and informative alternative to the public bus service.

🚌 Yas Express

This free shuttle bus links all the main attractions and amenities on Yas Island. The Yas Express also links Yas with Saadiyat Island.

🚲 Funride Bikes

One of the most popular ways of getting about the Corniche or Yas Island is by hiring a bike and riding along the dedicated cycle track. Funride cycle-hire stations are scattered about the city.

🚤 Water Taxis

Traditional water taxis, called *abras,* ply the waters of Al Maqta Khor, ferrying passengers for free from one five-star hotel to another and connecting with Souq Qaryat al Beri. In addition, the service now links to the hotel at the Eastern Mangroves, stopping at the Eastern Corniche on the way.

Abu Dhabi
Neighbourhoods

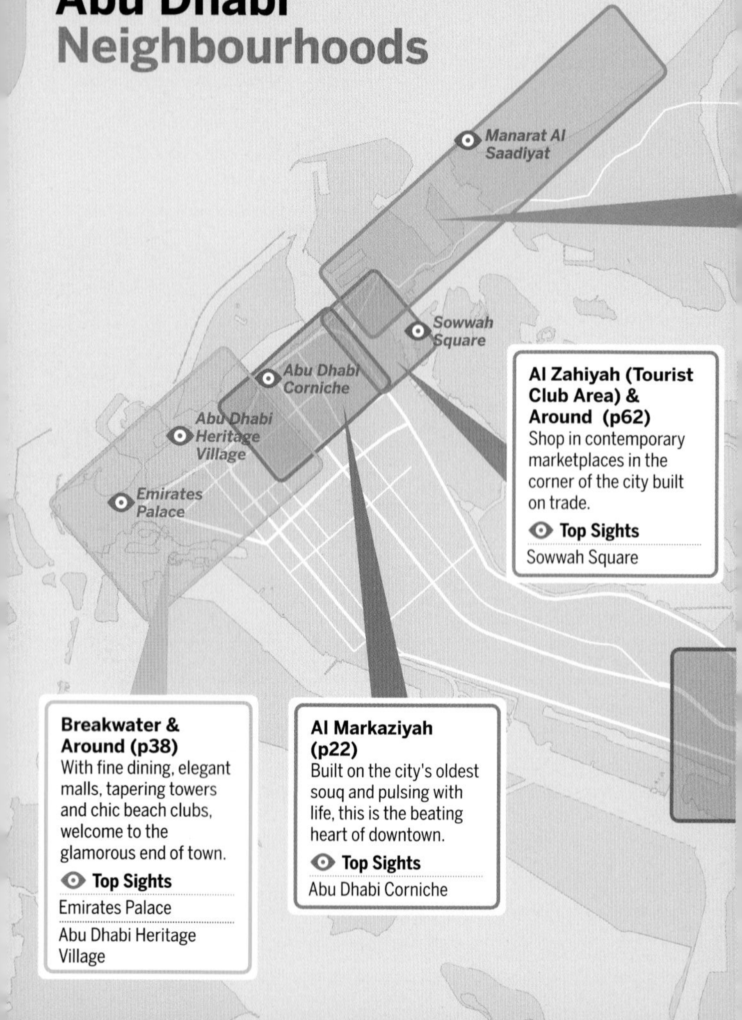

⊙ Manarat Al Saadiyat

⊙ Sowwah Square

⊙ Abu Dhabi Corniche

⊙ Abu Dhabi Heritage Village

⊙ Emirates Palace

Al Zahiyah (Tourist Club Area) & Around (p62)

Shop in contemporary marketplaces in the corner of the city built on trade.

⊙ **Top Sights**

Sowwah Square

Breakwater & Around (p38)

With fine dining, elegant malls, tapering towers and chic beach clubs, welcome to the glamorous end of town.

⊙ **Top Sights**

Emirates Palace

Abu Dhabi Heritage Village

Al Markaziyah (p22)

Built on the city's oldest souq and pulsing with life, this is the beating heart of downtown.

⊙ **Top Sights**

Abu Dhabi Corniche

Yas Island & Around (p102)
Home to UAE's Formula 1 circuit, Yas Island offers an exciting adrenalin rush or gentler pursuits in the neighbouring mangroves.

◉ Top Sights
Yas Marina Circuit

Masdar City

Al Mina & Saadiyat Island (p74)
Emirati people and their heritage feature in this culturally rich corner of the capital.

◉ Top Sights
Manarat Al Saadiyat

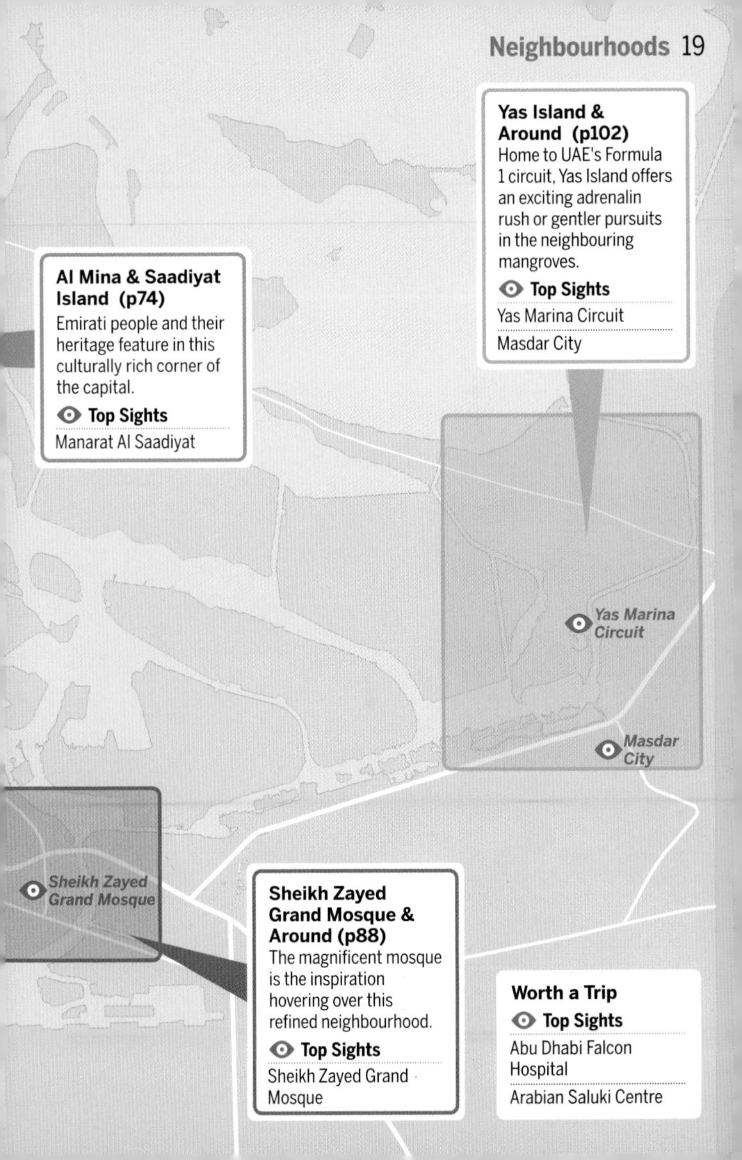

◉ *Yas Marina Circuit*

◉ *Masdar City*

◉ *Sheikh Zayed Grand Mosque*

Sheikh Zayed Grand Mosque & Around (p88)
The magnificent mosque is the inspiration hovering over this refined neighbourhood.

◉ Top Sights
Sheikh Zayed Grand Mosque

Worth a Trip
◉ Top Sights
Abu Dhabi Falcon Hospital

Arabian Saluki Centre

Explore
Abu Dhabi

Worth a Trip

Dome decoration in the Emirates Palace (p40)
LYUBOV TIMOFEYEVA/SHUTTERSTOCK ©

Explore

Al Markaziyah

Although Abu Dhabi has many vibrant districts, if you had to put your finger on the one that represents the city centre, then the area around Qasr Al Hosn, the city's oldest building, is surely it. The World Trade Centre is at the beating heart of this central district, appropriately built on the former site of the city's original souq.

The Sights in a Day

The centre of Abu Dhabi is clustered around **Qasr Al Hosn** (p30), the city's oldest building, and the World Trade Centre, one of its newest. Begin by taking stock of the district from the **Abu Dhabi Corniche** (p24). From here, **Burj Mohammed bin Rashid** (p30) towers over the city streets and dwarfs the giant **street sculpture** (p30) decorating the road island opposite.

Call into the **Souq Central Market** (p37) for a flavour of the ethnic diversity responsible for building a vibrant modern city at **Kababs & Kurries** (p35), which combines Indian and regional cuisines. Continue the cosmopolitan theme with an afternoon of shopping the souq's Persian Carpet House and Kashmir Cottage.

The evening is a good time to enjoy the downtown lights, including the **Etisalat** (p31) building with its golf ball crown. Night time is the right time, too, to bargain for bangles at the **Madinat Zayed Shopping & Gold Centre** (p36). Enjoy an evening with Moroccan food and Arab entertainment, including belly dancers, at the Millennium Hotel's **Marakesh** (p32) and end the night shaking your own booty at **Sax** (p36).

For a day enjoying local parks and cafes, see p26.

👁 Top Sights
Abu Dhabi Corniche (p24)

◯ Local Life
A Walk in the Park (p26)

🧡 Best of Abu Dhabi

Eating
Cho Gao (p27)

Zyara Café (p27)

Lebanese Flower (p32)

Al Ibrahimi Restaurant (p33)

Nightlife
Café Layali Zaman (p35)

Colombiano Coffee House (p27)

Tiara Resto Café (p36)

Stratos (p27)

Sax (p36)

Getting There

🚕 **Taxi** Most visitors use metered taxis to get around Al Markaziyah.

🚌 **Bus** Various buses service downtown but they're often crowded to board here.

🚌 **Big Bus** The tour bus stops on the Corniche by the Sheraton, the World Trade Centre, Al Hosn Fort and beside Al Markaziyah Gardens.

Top Sights
Abu Dhabi Corniche

The waterfront Corniche, with its white sandy beaches and generous promenade, stretches the entire length of the northwest shore of the city. Giving spectacular views of the high-rise tower blocks assembled along the seafront, it also offers one of the city's main recreation opportunities with beaches, a dedicated walking path and a separate cycle path weaving in and out of the Corniche's landscaped gardens. Little wonder that this seaboard road has become one of the top sights of the city.

◉ Map p28, A2

Abu Dhabi Corniche

Don't Miss

Between Skylines

Walk the Corniche and you get the odd sense that you are stepping along the crease between man-made verticals and nature's horizontals. Offering the best vantage point to review the dramatic inland skyline, the Corniche is punctuated with spectacular buildings such as the World Trade Centre, Nation Towers and Etihad Towers. They loom over the pavements, casting a welcome shadow on the flat-lining sea beyond.

Going the Distance

From end to end, the Corniche measures 8km and every inch of this beautifully landscaped promenade can be walked, cycled or skated. Along the route, scented tree jasmine, orange-flowering cordias, and pastel-blossomed tabebuias grace the flowerbeds, offering shaded respite from the heat.

Sun, Sea & Sand

For much of the year the waters of the Gulf are so calm and waveless they bear reflections like a lake. But that doesn't mean to say the sea is without moods: sometimes it is thick and viscous, like an oil slick, other times translucently clear. In the heat of summer, the humidity hovers visibly above the water and the Corniche sand is too hot to touch.

Fun for the Family

While the sea draws the attention of most visitors, the inland side of the Corniche is worth a visit too. Dotted with parks, play areas and *sheesha* cafes, it comes alive at night with local families seeking the sea breeze in the sweltering summer (May to September) or clustered around mobile heaters in winter (December to February).

☑ Top Tips

▸ Bicycles can be hired on the Corniche from Funride Sports (p68), near Beach Meydan.

▸ Towels and sunbeds are available from Bake Beaches in Al Markaziyah.

▸ There are two separate, enclosed public beaches with a nominal fee for women and families attended by a lifeguard.

▸ There are many shaded seating areas with sea views, making the promenade feasible most of the year.

▸ Carry water for the eastern Corniche.

✕ Take a Break

Pause for a snack at relaxing seafront Nova Beach Café (p124), near the public beaches of Meydan and Al Sahil.

Local Life
A Walk in the Park

The locals say, 'Walk Electra and Hamdan and you've walked the city'. Trace these parallel, frenetic east–west roads and you gain an instant sense of the bustling downtown. For something greener, however, and distinctly off the beaten track, the following route through some of the city's best parks and neighbouring watering holes offers a different perspective on the city centre.

❶ Park & Walk

Spread over three distinct areas – Al Nahyan Park, Family Park and Urban Park – **Al Markaziyah Gardens** (Corniche Rd (West); ⏱24hr) forms a broad band of recreational lawns parallel to the Corniche. These are the lungs of the city and, with their fountains and shaded seating, offer a great place to start a healthy constitutional.

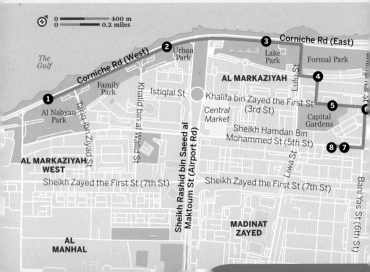

② Coffee Break

It may only be a couple of blocks, but reaching Urban Park from Al Nahyan Park will seem like an accomplishment for much of the year when heat competes with humidity to be the quintessential Gulf experience. Thankfully, sociable **Colombiano Coffee House** (☎02-633 7765; www.cchuae.com; Urban Park, Corniche Rd (West); ⊗8am-midnight) has comfortable waterside armchairs and delicious shots of energising espresso.

③ Monuments of Downtown

Pause at Al Itihad Square, with its impressive view of the city's CBD, before crossing into the next two shady parks straddling 4th Street. The centrepiece of **Lake Park** (Corniche Rd, East; admission free; ⊗24hr) is the 15m-high fountain and an open-air *sheesha* cafe. If you're still in garden mode, then continue on to Formal Park and take a turn in the maze.

④ Lebanese Lunch

Too much green? Let's change colour! Red is the overwhelming impression of **Zyara Café** (☎02-627 5006; Al Jazeera Tower, Corniche Rd (East); mains Dh50; ⊗8am-midnight), a fun little eatery popular with locals. Scarlet cushions, ruby drapes, carmine tablecloths and a whole medley of patterned fabrics make the interior a riot of colour.

⑤ Nap Time

You won't be the only one sleeping off lunch on a park bench in **Capital Gardens** (Muroor Rd, near Khalifa St; adult/child under 10yrs Dh1/free; ⊗8am-10pm Sun-Wed, to 11pm Thu-Sat). It's a favourite picnic spot and there's an erupting fountain giving a bit of lively respite during dead heat days.

⑥ Reviewing the Route

It's high time to review the route you've just travelled and **Stratos** (☎toll free 800 101 101; www.stratosabudhabi.com; Le Royal Méridien Abu Dhabi, 6th St; afternoon tea Dh149; ⊗3pm-2am Mon-Wed, to 3am Thu-Sat), a panoramic revolving lounge, is just the place to do it. Although the lounge can no longer command uninterrupted views, it does offer a fine high tea. Better still, opt for the tippling tea with champagne!

⑦ Join the City Social

Cho Gao (☎02-616 6101; www.ichotelsgroup.com; Crowne Plaza Abu Dhabi, Hamdan St; mains Dh70; ⊗noon-4pm & 7pm-1am) is a downtown favourite. There's always something happening – a work anniversary, a birthday, a girls' night out – making the pan-Asian restaurant feel more club than pub.

⑧ Under a Cloudless Sky

End the day in the Crowne Plaza's **Level Lounge** (☎02-616 6101; www.crowneplaza.com; Crowne Plaza Abu Dhabi, Hamdan St; cocktails from Dh40; ⊗6pm-2am). This relaxing open-air rooftop lounge offers a piece of tower-top calm in the middle of the hectic city. It's a good local haunt for *sheesha* and a chat with chill-out music.

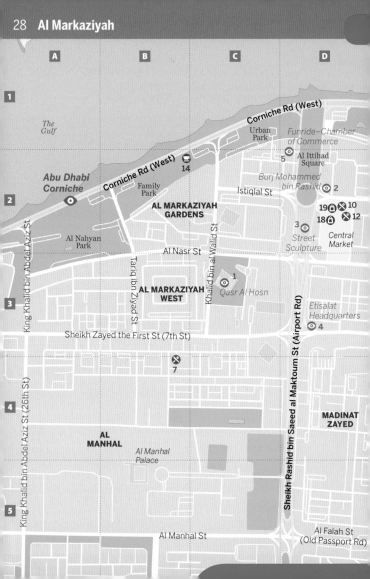

A   B   C   D

1

Corniche Rd (West)

The Gulf

Urban Park

Funride—Chamber of Commerce

5 ⊙ Al Ittihad Square

2

Corniche Rd (West)

Abu Dhabi Corniche

14 🍽

Family Park

AL MARKAZIYAH GARDENS

Istiqlal St

Burj Mohammed bin Rashid ⊙ **2**

19 🔒 ✕ **10**
18 🔒 ✕ **12**

Al Nahyan Park

Al Nasr St

3 ⊙
Street Sculpture

Central Market

King Khalid bin Abdel Aziz St

Tariq ibn Ziyad St

Khalid bin al Walid St

AL MARKAZIYAH WEST

1 ⊙
Qasr Al Hosn

Sheikh Rashid bin Saeed al Maktoum St (Airport Rd)

Etisalat Headquarters
⊙ **4**

3

Sheikh Zayed the First St (7th St)

✕
7

4

King Khalid bin Abdel Aziz St (26th St)

AL MANHAL

Al Manhal Palace

MADINAT ZAYED

5

Al Manhal St

Al Falah St
(Old Passport Rd)

E **F** **G** **H**

Corniche Rd (East)

Corniche Rd (East)

Sheraton Lagoon

🖵13

Lake Park

Lulu St

Formal Park

Umm al Nar St

1

2

AL MARKAZIYAH

16 ☆ 😣6

Khalifa bin Zayed the First St (3rd St)

Liwa St

😣11

Capital Gardens

😣15

Umm al Nar St

😣8

AL MARKAZIYAH

Al Salam St (8th St)

Sheikh Hamdan Bin Mohammed St (5th St)

Liwa St

3

Sheikh Zayed the First St (7th St)

17
🔒

East Rd (4th St)

😣9

Bani Yas St (6th St)

4

For reviews see	
🔵 Top Sights	p24
🔵 Sights	p30
😣 Eating	p32
🅿 Drinking	p35
☆ Entertainment	p36
🔒 Shopping	p36

5

Al Falah St

🧭

0 ———————— 400 m
0 ———————— 0.2 miles

Sights

Qasr Al Hosn
FORT

1 ⊙ Map p28, C3

Featured on the back of the Dh1000 note, and built on the site of a watchtower dating back to 1761 that safeguarded a precious freshwater well, this fort became the ancestral home of the ruling Al Nahyan family in 1793. The stone building seen today was constructed in the 20th century and served as the family's residence until 1966. After a brief spell as an administrative centre, the palace was closed in 1990 and has been undergoing long-term restoration ever since. (White Fort; Sheikh Zayed the First St)

Burj Mohammed bin Rashid
BUILDING

2 ⊙ Map p28, D2

This 92-floor giant (382m) among tower blocks forms part of the World

Q Local Life
Corniche Beach

There are three public beaches maintained by **Bake UAE** (www. bakeuae.com; Corniche Rd (West); adult/ child under 10 yrs Dh10/5; ⊗8am-8pm): one at Al Sahil for singles and groups, and two at Gates 3 and 4 for families shielded from view by a fence. Showers, changing rooms, cabanas, sunbeds and towels can be rented.

Q Local Life
Qasr Al Hosn Festival

Tipped to be an annual event, this **festival** (http://qasralhosnfestival. ae; Qasr Al Hosn, Zayed the First St; adult/child Dh10/free; ⊗4-11pm Feb, dates vary) is a celebration of UAE heritage. A series of workshops and guided tours of the old fort, currently under restoration, are included in the admission and a full program takes place in the adjoining Cultural Foundation Building.

Trade Centre and is an important landmark in this mixed-use development marking the middle of downtown. Not only is this Abu Dhabi's tallest building (at least for now) but it may just be unique in having an indoor terraced garden on the 90th floor! The tower is the tallest of two matching towers with distinctive sloping, elliptical roofs that look remarkable when lit at night. (World Trade Centre, 2nd St)

Street Sculpture
MONUMENTS

3 ⊙ Map p28, D2

There was a time when no self-respecting Gulf city would be seen without a giant concrete coffee pot. Those days have gone, for better or for worse, but a little reminder of the pioneering days of oil riches and the city development they brought can be seen in the traffic island between the World Trade Centre and Etisalat buildings.

MATILDE GATTONI/GETTY IMAGES ©

Qasr Al Hosn

The five concrete monuments show a date cover, incense burner, rosewater shaker, coffee pot and fort, symbolising the traditions of hospitality and Bedouin culture at the heart of Emirati life, together with the impulse to safeguard the land from marauding seafaring invaders.
(2nd & Khalifa Sts)

Etisalat Headquarters BUILDING

4 ◉ Map p28, D3

This iconic 27-floor building, with a 'golf ball' as its crowning glory, makes an excellent landmark for navigating the city's grid system. Built in 2001, it houses the headquarters of the local telephone service provider.
(cnr 7th & 2nd Sts)

Funride - Chamber of Commerce BICYCLE RENTAL

5 ◉ Map p28, D2

One of several stations for bike hire along the Corniche. If this is unstaffed, head for the main terminus outside the Hiltonia Beach Club at the far west end of the Corniche.
(☎02-556 6113; www.funridesports.com; Corniche Rd (West); per hr from Dh20; ☺4pm-midnight)

Eating

Marakesh
MOROCCAN $$$

 6 Map p28, F2

If the exotic Moroccan decor and the bona fide cuisine, including delicious *tajines* and couscous, aren't enough to bring you here, there's also an excellent Moroccan band, belly dancer and singer. Evenings here are memorable and go late.
(☑ ext 7334, 02-614 6000; www.millennium-hotels.ae; Millennium Hotel, Khalifa St; meals from Dh190; ⏱7pm-3am)

Lebanese Flower
LEBANESE $

 7 Map p28, B4

Amid a cluster of Middle Eastern snack, grill and pastry outlets, a short walk from Al Husn fort, this Lebanese restaurant is a local legend, attracting a multinational clientele of city residents. The generous plates of mezze include traditional favourites such as chicken livers, fried halloumi and tabouli and are excellent value. There's a pleasant family section upstairs. It's one block southeast of Zayed the First St.
(☑ 665 8700; near Zayed the First St; mains Dh25-50; ⏱7am-3am)

Understand
Smoking Sheesha

In Abu Dhabi, two sensations mark the hot and humid air of an Arabian evening: the wreaths of peach-scented smoke that spiral above the corner coffeehouses and the low gurgle of water, like a grumbling camel, in the base of a water pipe.

The habit of *sheesha* smoking, also known as hookah, narghile, argileh and hubble-bubble, originated hundreds of years ago in Persia and India.

Across the region, *sheesha* cafes are often a male affair: men lounge in ubiquitous white plastic chairs, indolently watching football on the TV, and occasionally breaking off from sucking and puffing to pass a word of lazy complaint to their neighbour or hail the waiter for hot coals.

In Abu Dhabi, however, these cafes attract mixed company. Here, women in black *abeyyas* (full-length robes) with sparkling diamante cuffs, drag demurely on velvet-clad mouthpieces, their smoking punctuating animated dialogue.

There is a popular misconception that because the smoke passes through water it is somehow filtered of toxins, but this is not the case. In fact, doctors argue it's worse for your health, not least because a typical *sheesha* session lasts for an hour and involves 200 puffs of nicotine, compared with only 20 for a regular cigarette.

Governments periodically try to prevent *sheesha* smoking, but the practice inevitably continues – an indispensable part of Arabian social life.

Street sculpture (p30) symbolising traditions of Bedouin culture

Automatic Restaurant LEBANESE $

8 Map p28, G3

Fresh shwarma, perfect hummus and whole heads of lettuce, raddish, rucola and pickles make this no-nonsense chain one of the most popular in the Gulf.

(☏02-676 9677; cnr Hamdan & 6th Sts; sandwiches Dh4-7, mains Dh18-65; ⊙11am-1am)

Al Ibrahimi Restaurant INDIAN $

9 Map p28, E4

This restaurant isn't going to win any prizes for decor but it does muster up delicious, authentic Indian and Pakistani dishes (particularly biryanis) and there is an outside seating area where life chaotically passes by.

(☏02-632 1100; www.ibrahimigroup.com; opposite Madinat Zayed Shopping & Gold Centre; biryani Dh30; ⊙11.30am-12.30am)

Shakespeare & Co INTERNATIONAL $$

10 Map p28, D2

The decor in this chintzy, Edwardian-style diner may not give you much indication of the Gulf location, but its popularity with Arab diners certainly will! Renowned as a favourite breakfast venue, there's a full English breakfast (with turkey sausage and beef bacon) on offer, or Lebanese-style crêpes.

(☏02-639 9626; www.shakespeare-and-co. com; ground fl, Souq Central Market; English breakfast from Dh54; ⊙7am-1pm)

Understand
Abu Dhabi's Pearl Heritage

Take a walk along Abu Dhabi's Breakwater and you'll come across a monument to the oyster – the mother of the pearl. Pearls are a common feature in Gulf cities because they formed a vital part of the region's former economy. In fact, for over four centuries the prosperity of the region was built on the collection and trading of these precious natural gems.

Creation of Pearls

Pearls are created when a grain of sand or grit enters the shell of an oyster, clam or mussel; the animal coats the intrusive irritant with a layer of nacre (mother-of-pearl) to make it smooth and less irksome. The longer the problem is nursed, the bigger it gets. Pearls are judged by the depth and quality of the lustre, the perfection of the shape and the colour, which naturally ranges from peach to iron.

Boom & Bust of the Pearling Industry

Despite the beauty of the catch, pearling was an unglamorous industry that entailed local 'divers' working with little more than a nose peg and a knife in shark-infested waters. They were hauled up with their bounty by 'pullers' working long and sun-baked shifts from June to October. At the height of the industry, thousands of dhows were involved in pearling along the Trucial Coast and loss of life was common.

Commercial pearling has long vanished from Gulf waters, thanks to a slump in the international pearl market in the 1930s alongside the development of the cultured pearl, pioneered in Japan. A cultured pearl is usually created through the artificial injection of grit, or more often a plastic bead, into the shell of an oyster. The uniformity of the bead generally guarantees a more uniform pearl and it is created in a much shorter space of time.

Thankfully, soon after the demise of the pearling industry, Abu Dhabi and neighbouring Emirates discovered oil – the black gold of the modern economy – but to this day, the locals have a soft spot for the oyster and its precious cargo can be seen adorning rings and necklaces in the Gold Centre.

Souq Central Market (p37)

La Brioche Café FRENCH $

11  Map p28, E2

A slice of Paris in the UAE, this mini-chain charmer makes healthy salads, bulging sandwiches and some of the best bread, croissants and pastries (baked fresh and local) in town. Service is swift and smiling, making this ideal for a takeaway to eat at Capital Gardens, which are almost opposite. (☑02-626 9300; www.labriocheuae.com; Khalifa St; mains Dh22-70)

Kababs & Kurries INDIAN $$

12  Map p28, D2

On the site of Abu Dhabi's original market, and located in the heart of Foster's attractive modern-day equiva-lent, you can imagine that Indian food has been served up on or near this spot for centuries. An extensive menu and outside terrace make this a refined and popular venue for a curry. (☑02-628 2522; ground fl, Souq Central Market, off Hamdan St; mains from Dh35)

Drinking

Café Layali Zaman SHEESHA CAFE

13  Map p28, E1

This family-friendly *sheesha* cafe serves snacks (Dh50) as well as coffee, though some may find the strong smell of *sheesha* over-pervasive. It is ever-popular with locals, particularly later at night. (☑02-627 7745; Lake Park, Corniche Rd, West; ⓢ9am-2am)

Tiara Resto Café
SHEESHA CAFE

 14 Map p28, B2

This smart little cafe in Urban Park, just across from the Corniche, offers seating 'in the round' – or at least arranged in a crescent. An outside terrace looks onto the park's fountains – a perfect spot for a late-night coffee and a chat with a friend in family-friendly company. *Sheesha* smoking is common here.

(Urban Park, Al Markaziyah Gardens, Corniche Rd (West); ⏱noon-midnight)

Sax
CLUB

15 Map p28, G2

In the early evening Sax lures chatty jet-setters huddled in intense tête-à-têtes, then cranks up the superb sound system to pack the dance floor with a glam-tastic, international crowd. Different promotions – Ladies' Night, Cabin Crew Night, Lebanese Weekend – keep things dynamic.

(☎02-674 2020; www.leroyalmeridienabu dhabi.com; Le Royal Méridien Abu Dhabi, 6th St; ⏱9pm-3.30am)

Entertainment

Cristal
LIVE MUSIC

16 Map p28, F2

A resident pianist provides genteel entertainment in the dapper Cristal. Dressed in polished oak and illuminated by candlelight and a fireplace, this is a haven of old-world charm in the heart of a frenetic city. Whisky and cigars are de rigueur for men, while the ladies sip on French champagne. For sophistication on the cheap, come during happy hour (5pm to 8pm).

(☎02-614 6000; www.milleniumhotels.ae; Khalifa St, Millennium Hotel; ⏱5pm-2am)

Shopping

Madinat Zayed Shopping & Gold Centre
GOLD SOUQ

 17 Map p28, E4

For first-time visitors to a gold souq, the window displays of bridal necklaces, earrings and belts, the trays of precious stones and the tiers of gold bangles are an attraction in their

Top Tip

Buying Gold

The jewellery in the Madinat Zayed Shopping & Gold Centre is not as prohibitive as it may look, despite the guaranteed gold (usually of around 23 karat) and the use of precious stones. When you buy bangles, necklaces and other items by weight, no extra cost is added for the complexity of design or the quality of the workmanship. Check the price of gold online before you go, and it will give you a rough idea of the expected price. In Islamic tradition, it is haram (forbidden by Islamic law) for men to wear gold – they usually wear silver!

own right. For those familiar with dazzling arrays of jewellery, Madinat Zayed Shopping & Gold Centre offers another reason to visit – affordable pearls set in gold necklaces and rings. (☎02-633 3311; www.madinatzayed-mall. com; 4th St; ⊙9am-11pm)

Souq Central Market   SOUQ

18 Map p28, D2

Norman Foster's reinterpretation of the traditional souq is a stylish composition of warm lattice woodwork, stained glass, walkways and balconies on the site of Abu Dhabi's historic central market. There are plenty of enticing stores here, including the Persian Carpet House & Antiques, Kashmir Cottage and the Chocolate Factory, and many boutiques selling perfumes and handicrafts. (☎02-810 7810; www.centralmarket.ae/souk; Khalifa St; ⊙10am-10pm Sun-Thu, to 11pm Fri & Sat)

World Trade Centre Mall   MALL

19 🔒 Map p28, D2

One of Abu Dhabi's newest malls, with lots of inaugural high-street and designer outlets. (☎02-508 2400; www.wtcad.ae; Hamdan St; ⊙10am-10pm Sun-Thu, to 11pm Fri & Sat)

Explore

Breakwater & Around

Still a big draw, the Emirates Palace holds its own in this glamorous neighbourhood dotted with relaxing beach clubs, but it has been joined by aerial attractions such as high tea at the Jumeirah and elevated shopping at the lofty St Regis. Back on earth, Abu Dhabi Heritage Village on Breakwater is a reminder of the city's humbler origins.

The Sights in a Day

☼ Expect some ups and downs today – thankfully lifts are available! Enjoy an early morning cycle along the Corniche to admire the city high-rises and then potter around the alternative shops of Al Khalidiyah, such as **Eclectic** (p59) and the **Folklore Gallery** (p59).

☼ Call in for a delicious early lunch at **Vasco's** (p45) under the terrace palms and then relax next door at either the **Nation Riviera Beach Club** (p44) or the public beach. Walk around or catch the bus to the **Heritage Village** (p42) and gain a perspective on the city's rapid development from *barasti* huts and pearl fishing to today's urban capital – best viewed from under the **giant flag** (p48). Call into the ever-popular **Marina Mall** (p61) to view the city from the **Sky Tower** (p48), or better still, ascend to the 74th floor of Jumeira at Etihad Towers for high tea at the **Observation Deck at 300** (p55).

☾ For a special occasion, book a special Emirati dinner at **Mezlai** (p53) in the sumptuous **Emirates Palace** (p40) followed by after-dinner drinks at **Etoiles** (p55).

For a local's day by the sea, see p44.

 Top Sights

The Emirates Palace (p40)

Abu Dhabi Heritage Village (p42)

 Local Life

A Nation of Seafarers (p44)

 Best of Abu Dhabi

Eating
Scott's (p51)

Vasco's (p45)

Sayad (p53)

Living Room Café (p52)

Al Asala Heritage Restaurant (p52)

Mezlai (p53)

Expat Haunts
Belgian Beer Café (p57)

Hemingway's (p57)

Getting There

🚌 **Bus** No 034 is one of several routes that connects Breakwater with the Corniche at Al Khalidiyah. No 009 connects Breakwater with Al Bateen.

🚌 **Big Bus** This tour bus connects the Corniche Beach, Heritage Village, Marina Mall and Etihad Towers.

Top Sights
Emirates Palace

What the Burj Khalifa in Dubai is to the vertical, the Emirates Palace is to the horizontal. With audacious domed gatehouses and flying ramps to the foyer, this vast hotel sits on a 1.3km private beach and dominates the end of the Corniche. You don't have to check in to check it out though, as it doubles as a cultural hub. For many residents, this is the first choice for celebrating a special occasion.

Map p46, B2

02-690 9000

www.emiratespalace. com

Corniche Rd (West)

Emirates Palace

Don't Miss

Architectural Style

At Emirates Palace there's far more of the 'Palace' than the 'Emirates'. Indeed, the enormous multi-winged, cupola-clad, red-stone building could be mistaken for a flight of 19th-century Orientalist fancy from Western Europe rather than anything distinctively Emirati. That's not a criticism: one rarely encounters such an ambitious horizontal building project these days.

The Statistics

Built at a cost of Dh11 billion, this is the BIG hotel in the Gulf. With 1002 crystal chandeliers hanging from 114 domes, nothing is done by halves here. The lights alone – stencilling the arches of all 302 luxury rooms, 40 suites, 16 palace suites and four presidential suites – are worth a visit.

Good as Gold

The Emirates Palace has a thing about gold. Not only is there a lobby ATM that dispenses solid gold bars, the precious metal also turns up in unexpected places. The signature 24kt cappuccino is sprinkled with it, the molten chocolate cake is a lava of gold, the camel burgers are packed in gold-dusted buns and you can even get yourself covered in the stuff.

A Cultural Icon

Hosting opera and renowned orchestras during the Abu Dhabi Classics concert season and showing screenings during the Abu Dhabi Film Festival, the Emirates Palace plays a regular part in the cultural expansion of the capital. It also houses the **Barakat Gallery**, which offers exquisite fine art from ancient China, Egypt, Africa, Greece and Rome.

☑ Top Tips

▶ You don't have to be a millionaire to stay at the Emirates Palace. Look for bargain packages in summer.

▶ Reserve high tea to avoid the minimum Dh100 charge levied on walk-in guests.

▶ Reservations are recommended for all restaurants.

▶ The concierge can book tickets, order a limousine...and arrange helicopter transfers.

▶ A kid's club helps entertain youngsters while ma and pa spa in peace!

✗ Take A Break

Not surprisingly, tempting breaks abound in the Emirates Palace. High tea at Le Café (p54) is a city institution – try the Arab version with a camelccino, made with camel's milk.

For something more substantial, Mezlai (p53) offers the most refined Emirati dishes in town.

Top Sights
Abu Dhabi Heritage Village

This reconstructed village provides an insight into life before oil in the UAE – a life that is still in evidence in many parts of the Arabian Peninsula to this day. The walled complex includes all the main elements of traditional Gulf life: a fort to repel invaders from the sea, a souq to trade goats for dates with friendly neighbours, and a mosque as a reminder of the central part that Islam plays in daily Arab life.

👁 Map p46

📞 02-681 4455

near Marina Mall, Breakwater

admission free

🕑 9am-5pm Sat-Thu, 3.30-9pm Fri

A potter demonstrating his craft at the Abu Dhabi Heritage Village

Don't Miss

Master Builders

Take a look at the *barasti* house, designed to catch the breeze through the palm frond uprights, and the wind tower that cooled air before the days of air-conditioning, and it becomes quickly apparent that the people of the Gulf were master builders, making the most of their scant resources.

Water Management the Ancient Way

To this day, water is a highly prized resource in the arid Gulf region and managing it is an important community responsibility. The ox-drawn well on display facilitated settled life while the ancient *falaj* (irrigation system) channelled water to crops that needed it, using stones to divert the flow.

Bedouin Blood

Most Emiratis proudly claim desert descent and while the nomadic life has largely disappeared from the UAE, many locals still like to return to their roots by camping in goat-hair tents similar to the ones on display in the Bedouin part of the village. Camels continue to play their role in the country's identity with many families owning a few in desert farms and attending regular races.

Crafts, New & Old

Spare some time to watch craftsmen at work in the tannery, glass-blowing workshop and swordsmiths. The *khanjar* (curved dagger) continues to be an important piece of ceremonial costume in neighbouring countries. Some fine old examples of these can be seen in the museum (inside the fort) alongside elaborate silver jewellery – another important traditional craft in the region.

☑ Top Tips

▶ Looking for a souvenir? Rice mats make good picnic blankets.

▶ Not that kind of souvenir? Mouse mats (mouse pads) with Oriental carpet designs are on sale in the village souq.

▶ Don't miss the pearl-diving paraphernalia in the museum.

▶ The *falaj* system is still used to water crops in the plantations of Al Ain and Liwa Oasis.

▶ Spare five minutes to see the photos from Abu Dhabi's early days in the museum dedicated to Sheikh Salem.

✗ Take a Break

In the middle of the village, Al Asala Heritage Restaurant (p52) provides a good opportunity to try traditional Emirati dishes such as minced shark.

To eat where the locals eat, try nearby Al Bateen Resort Yacht Club (p55) for uncomplicated Lebanese fare.

Local Life
A Nation of Seafarers

You can't claim to have visited Abu Dhabi if you haven't engaged with the sea in some way. The sea defines life here, whether as a reminder of seafaring heritage, as a place of play, as a 'must-have' view or as an increasingly important port and cruise destination. This seaboard route gives you a fish-eyed view of the neighbourhood.

❶ On the Best Bit of Beach
While the public beach is a great amenity, those in the know often head to the private beach clubs for a bit of value-added R&R. The **Nation Riviera Beach Club** (☎ 02-694 4444; www.nation rivierabeachclub.com; Corniche Rd (West); day use Sun-Thu Dh300, Fri & Sat Dh400), with steam room, sauna, Jacuzzi, watersports and a gym, offers plenty to do for those who just can't keep still. For those who can, the perfect

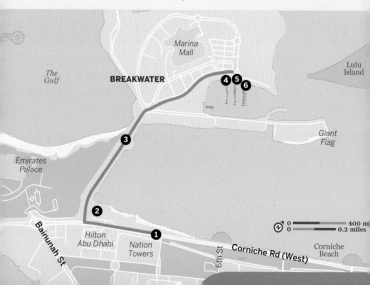

beach with an unruffled 200m shoreline offers a peaceful view of Breakwater and beyond.

❷ Seafood Lunch

Punctuate the seaboard experience with a seafood salad and glass of wine at the excellent **Vasco's** (☏ 02-692 4247; www.placeshilton.com/abu-dhabi; Corniche Rd (West); mains around Dh120; ⏱ noon-3.30pm & 7-11pm). The Vasco twist to the menu is a reminder of the early Portuguese influence in the region, who were protecting their coastal interests. While pirates are common in more southerly Arabian waters, there's little likelihood of a modern invasion from the sea – unless you count the ghost crabs.

❸ Swimming Against the Tide

It may not seem far, but for much of the year walking from the Hilton to the Marina can feel like a swim against the tide. And talking of tides, you may be lucky to see a red one – there's a natural blooming of blood-coloured algae common in the Gulf. At such times, many skip the swim and go for a *sheesha* instead. Thankfully, **Le Boulanger Marina Café** (☏ 02-681 8194; 18th St, Breakwater; mains from Dh90; ⏱ 8am-1am) is to hand!

❹ Desert Island

During your waterside amble, you'll have noticed the idyllic-looking island off the coast, Lulu Island. With its sandy beaches, date palms and dunes, it has risen like a mirage from the sea in one of the city's many ambitious tourism projects. Not yet officially open to the public, many pitch up for an ad hoc picnic on the reclaimed land. Check with **Lulu Boats** (☏ 050-642 9777; www.luluboats. com; Marina, Breakwater; from around Dh150) for a ride over.

❺ Viewing Progress

It's probably close to sunset by now, so head to the **Havana Café & Restaurant** (☏ 02-681 0044; Marina, Breakwater; sheesha from Dh35; ⏱ 7am-2pm) for a mixed fruit sundowner. With one of the very best views of nighttime Abu Dhabi, the outside terrace at this half hidden but highly popular *sheesha* cafe is always teeming with appreciative puffers, smokers and gurglers. The service is attentive despite the crowds and, best of all, you can see where you've just walked from the comfort of an armchair.

❻ Seafood Supper Aboard the Shuja

Our local interest route has taken us in the sea, by the sea, and provided plenty of views of the sea. It's now time to cruise across it. Operated through Le Royal Méridien Abu Dhabi, the elegant luxury yacht **Shuja** (☏ 02-674 2020; Marina, Breakwater; brunch Dh350-500) plies the placid waters on a number of short bay cruises, leaving from the marina on Breakwater. The dinner cruise includes a fresh seafood buffet.

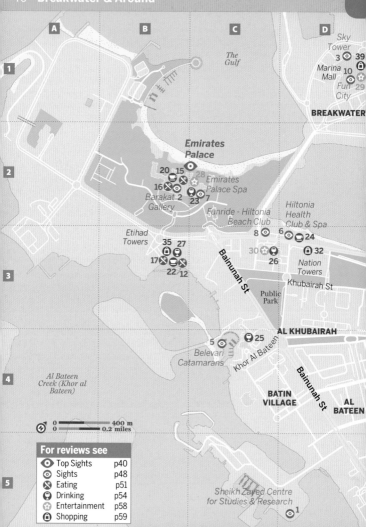

A · B · C · D

Sky Tower
3 · 39
Marina Mall · 10
Fun City · 29

The Gulf

BREAKWATER

Emirates Palace

20 · 15 · 28
16 · Emirates Palace Spa
Barakat Gallery · 23 · 7

Funride - Hiltonia Beach Club
Hiltonia Health Club & Spa
8 · 6 · 24

Etihad Towers
35 · 27
17 · 30 · 26 · 32
22 · 12
Nation Towers

Bainunah St
Khubairah St

Public Park

AL KHUBAIRAH

5 · 25
Belevari Catamarans
Khor Al Bateen

Bainunah St

BATIN VILLAGE

AL BATEEN

Al Bateen Creek (Khor al Bateen)

0 —— 400 m
0 —— 0.2 miles

Sheikh Zayed Centre for Studies & Research

1

E F G H

Lulu Island

Abu Dhabi
Helicopter
Tour

21

9

Abu Dhabi Heritage Village

4 UAE Flagpole

14

The Gulf

Family Park

Corniche Rd (West)

Corniche Beach

18

AL MARKAZIYAH GARDENS

Al Nahyan Park

Corniche Rd (West)

Al Nasr St

19

32

6th St

Al Khalidiyah Kid's Park

Al Khaleej al Arabi St

King Khalid bin Abdel Aziz St

Tariq ibn Ziyad St

Sheikh Zayed the First St (7th St)

34 33

31

11

13th St

19th St

Sultan bin Zayed the First St

Al Khalidiyah Public Park

37

AL KHALIDIYAH

38

13

36

AL MANHAL

Al Manhal Palace

King Khalid bin Abdel Aziz St (26th St)

Al Manhal St (9th St)

Al Khaleej al Arabi St

Bainunah St

Al Karamah St (24th St)

Sights

Sheikh Zayed Centre for Studies & Research
MUSEUM

1 Map p46, D5

This eclectic collection of artefacts and personal memorabilia documents the life of Sheikh Zayed, the founding father of the Emirates. The collection is housed in a rare assembly of old villas sporting traditional wind towers, on the coast near the new Al Bateen developments. The museum complex, complete with 'Baba' (Father) Zayed's favourite blue Mercedes and beat-up Land Rover, is looking unloved, perhaps in anticipation of the new national museum on Saadiyat Island. (Baba Zayed's House; off Bainunah St, Al Bateen; admission free; ⏱8am-3pm Sun-Thu)

Barakat Gallery
GALLERY

2 Map p46, B2

This exclusive private gallery, with branches in Beverly Hills, Los Angeles and Mayfair, London, houses some exquisite artefacts. With a heritage of over 100 years as art dealers, the family-run business has contributed pieces to museums, corporations and private collections around the world. (✆02-690 8950; www.barakatgalleryuae.com)

Sky Tower
VIEWPOINT

3 Map p46, D1

You may pay a bit extra for a burger, sandwich or salad in the aerial Colombiano Coffee House (p27) at the top of this observation tower but there's no charge for the panoramic view from 360 degrees' worth of windows. If you'd rather not walk round the view yourself, head for Tiara (p36), the revolving restaurant upstairs. (✆02-681 9009; Marina Mall, Breakwater; admission free; ⏱10am-10pm)

UAE Flagpole
LANDMARK

4 Map p46, F2

At 122m this giant flagpole was the tallest free-standing flagpole in the world when it was constructed in 2001. It lost its title to the Raghadan Flagpole in Jordan in 2004 and is now a long way short of the world's tallest. That said, the Emirati flag makes a fine landmark and the small promenade beneath the pole offers one of the best photo opportunities in the city for an uninterrupted view of the skyline. It's near the Abu Dhabi Heritage Village.

Belevari Catamarans
CRUISE

5 Map p46, C4

A chance to board Abu Dhabi's largest catamaran, a 22.5m, 11m-wide luxury boat, on a 2½-hour cruise with soft drinks, snacks and music included. (✆02-643 1494; http://belevari.com; InterContinental, Bainunah St, Al Bateen; adult/child Dh350/250; ⏱5pm Thu)

The UAE Flagpole, near the Abu Dhabi Heritage Village

Hiltonia Health Club & Spa

BEACH

6 ◎ Map p46, D3

This recommended beach club occupies prime position at the western end of the Corniche. Set in beautifully landscaped gardens alongside a white-sand beach shaded by palm trees, the club offers a variety of watersports, three swimming pools, a gym and cafe. Punctuate a lazy day with a seafood salad and glass of wine at the excellent restaurant, Vasco's (p45). (📞02-692 4247; Corniche Rd (West); adult/child Fri & Sat Dh195/90, Sun-Thu Dh150/70; ⏰8am-8pm)

Emirates Palace Spa

SPA

7 ◎ Map p46, C2

For the ultimate indulgence, enquire about the three-hour gold ritual. This includes a 24kt-gold facial, an application of gold from head to toe and a massage using gold shea butter. If you don't come out feeling like Tutankhamun's mummy, it won't be for want of trying! Prices on request (sit down first). (📞02-690 7978; www.kempinski.com; Emirates Palace)

Big Bus Abu Dhabi
BUS TOUR

For an informative introduction to the city, this hop-on hop-off service is hard to beat. The route lasts 90 minutes and passes all the major sights, including Sheikh Zayed Grand Mosque, the Corniche, the Heritage Village and the Emirates Palace. Tickets, which include free headphones, are available online, from hotels and from kiosks next to the Big Bus stops.
(📞02-449 0026; www.bigbustours.com; tickets 24hr adult/child Dh200/100, 48hr adult/child Dh260/130; ⊗9am-7pm)

Funride - Hiltonia Beach Club
CYCLING

8 Map p46, C3

A great way to appreciate the modern skyline of Abu Dhabi's western shore is to cycle the dedicated bike path along the Corniche. Bicycles (men's, women's and children's) are available for rent at four stations along the road, with the most reliably staffed station at the far western end of the road, near the Hiltonia Beach Club.
(📞02-441 3264; www.funridesports.com; Corniche Rd (West); per hr adult/child Dh30/20; ⊗6.30am-midnight)

Understand
Thank Goodness for GPS

Whether you're looking for Sheikh Zayed the First St, 7th Street or Electra Street will largely depend on what map you're using! The initiative to rename the city's roads (a term used interchangeably with 'streets') from the former numbering system has resulted in confusion, especially as some districts have been renamed too (including 'Tourist Club Area', now known as Al Zahiyah).

Currently main roads are named after prominent Emirati figures while smaller roads reflect places. As former and current names are still common currency, here's a list of the main roads and their alternate names:

Sheikh Rashid Bin Saeed Al Maktoom 2nd, Airport

Sultan bin Zayed the First 4th, East, Muroor, New Airport

Fatima bint Mubarak St 6th, Umm Al Nar, Bani Yas, Baniyas

Sheikh Zayed bin Sultan 8th, Al Salam, East Coast, Eastern Ring, New Corniche

Khalifa bin Zayed the First 3rd, Khalifa, Sheikh Khalifa Bin Zayed, Al Istiqalal

Sheikh Hamdan Bin Mohammed 5th, Hamdan, Al Nasr, Al Khubairah

Sheikh Zayed the First 7th, Electra

Al Falah 9th, Old Passport Rd

Abu Dhabi Helicopter Tour

SCENIC FLIGHTS

9 Map p46, E1

Abu Dhabi, with its many spectacular buildings, islands and expanses of mangrove may look inspiring from the Big Bus tour but it takes on a whole different perspective from the air. Rising vertically above the marina but finding yourself at eye-level with a middle floor of a tower block is one way to gauge the full height of the city's achievements. (☑04-294 6060; http://abudhabihelicopter tour.com; Marina Mall Terminal; 20/30min flight Dh3350/5000 for 6 passengers; ☺by appointment)

Fun City

RIDES

10 Map p46, D1

Offering games and rides for pre-teens, the Fun City brand is a favourite with children across Gulf countries. (☑02-681 5527; www.funcity.ae; Marina Mall, Breakwater; various packages available from around Dh50; ☺10am-10pm)

Al Khalidiyah Public Park

PARK

11 Map p46, F4

One of many popular, shady parks in Abu Dhabi, this park offers a respite from the heat of the Corniche in the summer months. There's a jogging track (20-minute circuit) and a variety of climbing frames and other attractions for youngsters. (Khalidiyah Garden; between 16th & 30th (Al Khaleej al Arabi) Sts; adult/child Dh1/free; ☺24hr)

Local Life
Henna Salons

Before a wedding or party, Gulf ladies paint elaborate designs in henna on their hands and feet. The use of henna (made from the leaves of *Lawsonia inermis* mixed to a paste with essential oils) is centuries old and associated with sensuality. It takes three hours for the henna to dry, lasts for 10 days and costs around Dh50. Enjoy participating in this local custom at:

Cassablanca Ladies Salon (☑02-634 4505; www.casablanca.ae; off Sheikh Zayed the First St; ☺9am-9pm Sat-Thu)

Beautiful Henna Centre (☑02-634 3963; www.beautifulhennacentre.com; Airport Rd; ☺9.30am-9pm Sat-Thu, 10am-9pm Fri)

Eating

Scott's

SEAFOOD $$$

12 Map p46, B3

Although related to the famous London restaurant of the same name and carrying many of its signature dishes, the chargrilled kingfish and the salt-baked Sultan Ibrahim is caught locally from the Gulf. The blue-lit, oyster-shaped architecture is appropriate to the gems served up from this award-winning restaurant. It has a romantic outdoor terrace and extravagant sea views. (☑02-811 5666; Jumeirah at Etihad Towers; mains around Dh120; ☺noon-3.30pm & 6.30-11pm)

Living Room Café

CAFE $

13 Map p46, G4

This award-winning, family-run venue started life as a coffee-and-cake experience and has grown by word of mouth into a much-beloved restaurant. With an emphasis on family-friendly fare (including a VIP children's menu and kid's corner), the home-baked cakes, all-day breakfasts, toasted sandwiches and healthy salads will especially please those with a craving for something out of mum's kitchen. It's inside the Sarouh Compound.

(☑02-639 6654; www.thelivingroomcafe abudhabi.com; Khalifa bin Shakhbout (28th) St; light meals around Dh10; ☑7.30am-11.30pm Sun-Thu, 8am-11.30pm Fri & Sat)

Al Asala Heritage Restaurant

EMIRATI $$

14 Map p46, E2

Offering traditional *jasheed* (minced shark) and *harees* (meat and wheat 'porridge'), and *umm ali* (Arab bread pudding) in the Heritage Village, this restaurant, with its fine view of the Abu Dhabi skyline, caters mainly for tour groups sampling the buffet as

---

Understand
Regional Menu Decoder

Al Khalidiyah, Breakwater and Al Bateen are three of the best districts to try some of Abu Dhabi's best regional foods. By 'best', we mean not just the most inventive uses of local ingredients (laban, goat meat and camel's milk) in fine-dining restaurants. We also mean the most delicious traditional fare in cheap and cheerful restaurants found near Sheikh Zayed the First St in Al Khalidiyah.

In the more local haunts, descriptions of dishes are not always available and English may be limited, so here's a quick primer to help with the menu:

baba ghanooj smoked aubergine dip

kibbeh minced lamb, bulgur wheat and pine nut patty

harees slow-cooked wheat and lamb

mandi baked chicken and rice

madfoon slow-baked lamb on rice with chilli sauce

shwarma compressed meat grilled on a vertical spit, garnished and rolled in Arabic bread

kunafa parcels of sweet cheese dipped in syrup

umm ali bread-based pudding with sultanas, nuts and nutmeg

SIMON REDDY/ALAMY ©

Harees, a traditional meat and wheat 'porridge'

part of their cultural tour. If unaccompanied by a tour guide you'll be attentively looked after. (☏02-681 2188; www.alasalahrestaurants. com; mains Dh60, buffet Dh75; ☺noon-4pm daily, buffet 1-5pm & 6.30-9pm Fri)

Mezlai
EMIRATI $$$

15 ✗ Map p46, B2

Meaning 'old door lock', Mezlai delivers a rare chance to enter the world of local flavours. The Emirati food is prepared from organic and locally sourced ingredients. Favourites include hammour *mafrook* (a whitefish spread served with fresh bread) and lamb *medfoun* (shoulder of lamb, slow-cooked in a banana leaf). The

potato mashed with camel's milk makes an interesting side dish. (☏02-690 7999; www.kempinski.com; 1st fl, Emirates Palace; mains Dh110-205; ☺1pm-10.30pm)

Sayad
SEAFOOD $$$

16 ✗ Map p46, B2

Serving the city's finest seafood in a striking aquamarine setting (quite a contrast to the traditional marble and silk of the surrounding Emirates Palace), Sayad has earned a reputation as a top choice for a special occasion. Dishes are imaginative, such as the lobster salad with watermelon and mango. Reservations are essential. (☏02-690 7999; www.emiratespalace.com;

Emirates Palace, Ras Al Akhdar; mains Dh150-200; ⏱6.30-11.30pm)

Brasserie Angélique FRENCH $$$

17 Map p46, B3

It may seem perverse to recommend a French restaurant in the capital city of the Emirates, but this award-winning French fine-dining restaurant, which only opened in 2013, has taken the city by storm. The chandeliers are thoroughly Gulf but the food is thoroughly Gallic with foie gras, escargots and bouillabaisse headlining the chef's menu. (☑02-811 5666; www.jumeirah.com; Jumeirah at Ethihad Towers; mains Dh150; ⏱noon-3.30pm & 7-11.30pm)

Nova Beach Café CAFE $

18 Map p46, F3

One of the few public places to have a coffee and light bite overlooking

the sea, this cafe has a devoted local following. If you're walking or cycling the Corniche, or looking for a snack between swims, this is a sociable venue where you can catch the sea breeze. (☑02-658 1879; Corniche Rd (West); snacks around Dh40; ⏱noon-10.30pm)

Café Du Roi FRENCH $

19 Map p46, F3

With professional coffee and delicious pastries, croissants and sandwiches, plus seven choices of fluffy filled omelettes, this French-style cafe is the perfect spot for some leisurely lingering. There's also a branch at Abu Dhabi Mall. (☑02-681 5096; Corniche Rd (West); mains Dh15-35; ⏱7am-midnight; 🛜)

Drinking

Le Café HIGH TEA

20 Map p46, B2

Try an Arabic twist on the classic English high tea with mezze, Arabic savoury pastry and baklava with a camelccino made with camel's milk or a cappuccino sprinkled with 24kt gold flakes. High tea of both classic and Arab variety is practically an institution at the Emirates Palace so book in advance to avoid the minimum spend fee of Dh100 per person. (☑02-690 7999; www.emiratespalace.com; Emirates Palace, Corniche Rd (West); high tea from Dh278; ⏱high tea 2-6pm)

Sayad (p53) in the Emirates Palace (p40)

Al Bateen Resort Yacht Club
SHEESHA CAFE

21 Map p46, E1

Serving a variety of tasty fruit juices and basic Lebanese dishes, this is a very popular place to enjoy an evening of alfresco *sheesha* in the company of locals.
(02-222 2886; near Marina Mall; fresh fruit juice Dh20; 24hr)

Observation Deck at 300
CAFE

22 Map p46, B3

This chic coffee shop on the 74th floor of the iconic Jumeirah at Etihad Towers hotel serves the highest high tea in Abu Dhabi with a sublime panorama of city, sea and surrounds. The '300' refers to the metres above ground.
(02-811 5666; www.jumeirah.com; Tower 2, Level 74, Jumeirah at Etihad Towers; entry Dh75, incl Dh50 for food or drink, high tea Dh175; 10am-6pm)

Etoiles
BAR

23 Map p46, C2

Don those killer heels, gals, slick back the hair, chaps, and join the super-chic crowd at this achingly stylish late-night bar. It's perfect for post-dinner drinks.
(02-690 8960; www.etoilesuae.com; Emirates Palace, Corniche Rd (West), Ras Al Akhdar; 11pm-4am Mon-Fri)

Understand
The Bedouin Heart of Emirati Culture

Visit the Abu Dhabi Heritage Village in Breakwater and you'll be sure to find Emirati visitors clustered around the camel enclosure and the Bedouin tent. They may belong to an urbane and urban generation but the capital's citizens are quick to claim Bedouin roots.

Today's Modern Bedouin
There are few Bedouin in the UAE who live up to their name as true desert nomads these days, but there are still communities who live a semi-traditional life on the fringes of the Empty Quarter. Their survival skills in a harsh terrain and their ability to adapt to changing circumstances are part of their enduring success. Most of today's Bedouin have modernised their existence with 4WD trucks (it's not unusual to find the camel travelling by truck these days), fodder from town and purified water from bowsers (water tankers). All these features have limited the need to keep moving. Some have mobile phones and satellite TV and most listen to the radio. Many no longer move at all.

Old Habits Die Hard
Despite changes to their living experience, Bedouin remain the proud people of the desert and many of their customs and values, dating from the earliest days of Islam, remain unchanged. They rear livestock and trade with fellow tribespeople. Some live in goat-hair tents with the women's harem curtained off. The men's section serves as the public part of the house where guests are shown hospitality, an enduring feature of the Bedouin tradition. It's here that all the news and gossip – a crucial part of successful survival in a hostile environment – is passed on.

Mutual Benefit
Part of the ancient Bedouin creed is that no traveller in need of rest or food should be turned away. Likewise, a traveller assumes the assured protection of his hosts for a period of three days and is guaranteed a safe passage through tribal territory. Such a code of conduct traditionally ensured the survival of all in a difficult environment with scant resources. Even today, a city host will walk a guest to the front gate, symbolic of this ancient custom.

Observation Deck at 300 (p55)

Arabic Café

SHEESHA CAFE

24 Map p46, D3

If you are tempted to while away the evening the local way with a puff of *sheesha,* a sip of coffee, a fresh fruit juice and good conversation with a friend, then this is a sheltered venue to try it out for size before hitting the real thing on pavements across town. (☎02-681 1900; Hilton Abu Dhabi, Corniche Rd (West); ⏰8am-10pm Thu & Fri, to 11.30pm Sat-Wed)

Belgian Beer Café

BAR

25 Map p46, C4

Not convinced there's more to beer than a canned lager? Head to the Belgian Beer Café, overlooking the

marina at the InterContinental, and the 18 specialist draughts and bottles behind the bar may just convince you otherwise. Follow the expat lead and order *frites* (fries) with a very Belgian pot of mussels – reputedly the best in town. (☎02-666 6888; www.belgianbeercafe.com; InterContinental Hotel, Bainunah St, Khor al Bateen; ⏰5pm-1am)

Hemingway's

BAR

26 Map p46, C3

A cantina popular with long-term expats, Hemingway's is the place to lounge in front of the big screen for beer, chips (albeit nacho chips) and football. There's a live band from

Monday to Saturday, Ladies' Night is on Tuesday and Sunday is Quiz Night.
(📞02-681 1900; www.abudhabi.hilton.com; Hilton Abu Dhabi, Corniche Rd (West); ⏰noon-1am)

Ray's Bar   BAR

27 🍺 Map p46, B3

For a sense of the sheer audacity of Abu Dhabi's architectural vision, a visit to the Etihad Towers is a must. Arrive at sunset and be dazzled by the light bouncing off the outside of these spectacular towers. The elegant and intimate bar on the lofty 62nd floor is currently the 'top' spot in town – measured in metres!
(📞02-811 5555; www.jumeirah.com; Jumeirah at Etihad Towers; ⏰5pm-2am)

Local Life

Centre of Original Iranian Carpets

The galleries of Gulf cities offer the perfect chance to buy a Persian carpet. At this **carpet centre** (Map p46, F3; 📞02-681 1156; www.coicco.com; off Al Khaleej al Arabi St; ⏰9.30am-1.30pm & 5-9.30pm Sat-Thu), spread over three floors, there are over 4000 carpets to choose from. There is a useful buyers guide and glossary on the shop's detailed website.

Entertainment

Abu Dhabi Classics   CLASSICAL MUSIC

28 ⭐ Map p46, C2

This concert series brings top classical performances – including renowned international soloists and famous orchestras – to the city throughout a season lasting from October to the end of May. Venues include the Emirates Palace Auditorium, Manarat Al Saadiyat, a floating stage off the Breakwater during the Volvo Ocean Race, and some historical sites in Al Ain.
(📞toll free 800 555; www.abudhabiclassics.com; Emirates Palace; tickets Dh30-400)

Vox Cinemas   CINEMA

29 ⭐ Map p46, D1

Showing 3D and 4D films as well as a full repertory of new releases, Vox Cinemas can be booked online.
(📞02-681 8464; www.voxcinemas.com; Marina Mall; tickets from Dh47)

Jazz Bar & Dining   LIVE MUSIC

30 ⭐ Map p46, C3

Cool cats flock to this sophisticated supper club that serves contemporary fusion cuisine in a modern art deco–inspired setting. But the venue is less about the food and more about the music – jazz bands play on a stage to an audience of sagely nodding aficionados.
(📞02-681 1900; www.abudhabi.hilton.com; Hilton Abu Dhabi, Corniche Rd (West); mains Dh50-200; ⏰7pm-12.30am Sat-Mon, to 1.30am Tue-Fri)

Avenue at Etihad Towers (p60)

Shopping

Paris Avenue
FASHION

31 🔒 Map p46, G4

A favourite boutique that trends with the latest fashionable accessories from young graduate designers from Europe.
(📞02-653 4030; www.parisavenue.ae; off Zayed the First St, near Al Khalidiyah Mall; ⏰10am-8pm)

Nation Galleria
MALL

32 🔒 Map p46, D3

This new shopping experience is not just your average mall – it houses many unique stores, extravagant eateries and a huge Wafi Gourmet, the celebrated Lebanese restaurant chain.
(📞02-681 8824; Nation Towers, Corniche Rd (West))

Folklore Gallery
ART

33 🔒 Map p46, G4

An opportunity to invest in a piece by up-and-coming local resident artists from a shop that started life mainly as a framing service in 1995.
(📞02-666 0361; www.folkloregallery.net; Zayed the First St)

Eclectic
ANTIQUES

34 🔒 Map p46, F4

A delightful browsing experience with old furniture and textiles hobnobbing with new paintings, ceramics and sculpture by local Gulf artists. (📞02-666 5158; Zayed the First St; ⏰10.30am-1.30pm & 5-9pm Sat-Thu)

Avenue at Etihad Towers   FASHION

35 🔒 Map p46, B3

Designer-led, luxury fashion items in an exclusive, opulent venue; this is boutique shopping at its finest. (📞toll free 800 384 4238; www.avenueatetihadtowers.ae; Etihad Towers, Corniche Rd West)

Al Khalidiyah Mall   MALL

36 🔒 Map p46, G4

The essential, if rather uninspiring, expat shopping experience, especially for the those from the UK.

(📞02-635 4000; www.khalidiyamall.com; Khalid bin Adbel Aziz/26th St; ⏰10am-10pm Sun-Wed, to 11pm Thu & Sat)

Abu Dhabi Pottery Establishment   CERAMICS

37 🔒 Map p46, F4

A showcase for the collectable ceramics of Homa Vafaie-Farley, the venue also doubles as a pottery workshop with classes on offer. (📞02-666 7079; www.abudhabipottery.com; 16th St; ⏰9am-1pm & 4.30-9pm Sat-Thu)

Ghaf Gallery   ART GALLERY

38 🔒 Map p46, F4

One of only two private galleries devoted to modern art in Abu Dhabi,

BRENT WINEBRENNER/GETTY IMAGES ©

Marina Mall

the Ghaf Gallery is a beautiful little exhibition space in the heart of Al Khalidiyah. The gallery, which is the brainchild of Mohammed Kanoo, a Bahraini artist and patron, and local Emirati artist, Jalal Luqman, comes into its own during the Abu Dhabi Festival when it showcases the work of artists in residence.
(☏02-665 5332; ghafgallery@gmail.com; Al Khaleej al Arabi St; admission free; ☺10am-9pm Sat-Thu)

Marina Mall MALL

39 🔒 Map p46, D1

For locals, the main draw of this big mall on the Breakwater seems to be IKEA, but fortunately there are over 400 other stores in case you don't need yet another Billy bookcase. Entertainment options include a multiplex cinema, tiny ice-skating rink and Fun City (p51), a huge activity centre for children that includes a (relatively tame) roller coaster and dodgem cars.
(☏02-681 2310; www.marinamall.ae; Breakwater; ☺10am-10pm Sat-Wed, to 11pm Thu, 2-11pm Fri)

Explore

Al Zahiyah (Tourist Club Area) & Around

Welcome to the mall quarter of the capital, where old and new shopping districts straddle Al Zahiyah and the burgeoning developments of Al Maryah Island. This is a neighbourhood where shopping remains king, whether you've come looking for Arabian prawns for supper, a pot to cook them in or designer plates to serve them on.

The Sights in a Day

☀ Start with a morning constitutional in **Heritage Park** (p68) with its fine views of the old dhow harbour and then call in for a game of backgammon at **Planet Café** (p71). Malls aplenty spring up across the city but dedicated shoppers keep flocking back to **Abu Dhabi Mall** (p72), a favourite for fashion. There are lots of local twists here, with **Jashanmal** (p73), the Gulf's answer to the department store, and **Grand Stores** (p73), where you can buy a miniature silver oil rig model or a marble falcon. Arabian sweet and date stores, *abeyya* shops and *oud* perfumers will ensure you won't forget where you are.

☀ Garner some energy for more shopping with lunch at **Automatic** (p69), the best-selling chain of Lebanese restaurants. Browse the small craft outlets in the nearby **Khalifa Centre** (p73), where leather camels and bone boxes, *sheesha* bottles and hand-loomed carpets make popular souvenirs.

★ Dine at the elegant **Galleria** (p73) on Al Maryah Island, across the water from Al Zahiyah, and wander along the **promenade** (p67) pondering the evolution of shopping from its humble port-side origins.

 Top Sights

Sowwah Square (p64)

💜 **Best of Abu Dhabi**

Nightlife

Ally Pally Corner (p69)

Bentley Bistro & Bar (p69)

Planet Café (p71)

Entertainment

49er's The Gold Rush (p71)

Grand Cinemas Abu Dhabi (p72)

Shopping

Abu Dhabi Mall (p72)

Khalifa Centre (p73)

Galleria (p73)

Getting There

🚌 **Bus** Many bus routes stop outside Abu Dhabi Mall, the city's airport bus terminus. Bus No 5 links Abu Dhabi Mall with Sowwah Sq, outside the Galleria on Al Maryah Island.

🚌 **Big Bus** This tour bus stops outside Abu Dhabi Mall and links Al Zahiyah with Saadiyat Island and the Sheraton on the Corniche.

Top Sights
Sowwah Square

At the heart of Al Maryah Island's new urban development is Sowwah Square, on the cutting edge of modern town planning. Home to some of the city's most exciting new buildings, it encompasses the sophisticated Rosewood Abu Dhabi hotel and glamorous Galleria mall. From the square's adjacent promenade are striking views across the water towards Al Zahiyah, while various feats of engineering vie for attention, including the Maryland Clinic with its catwalk podium and the island's new suspension bridge.

👁 Map p66, D4

www.sowwahsquare.ae

Al Maryah Island

The Galleria mall in Sowwah Square

Don't Miss

The Birth of Abu Dhabi's New CBD

With the construction of the new stock exchange, Sowwah Square is set to become the new central business district of Abu Dhabi. The area is already taking shape, built on 57 hectors of island that first had to be elevated 14m above sea level. The island will offer a rare freehold opportunity for non-Emirati investors to build for the future, as part of Abu Dhabi's 2030 plan for sustainable development.

A Walkable Solution

The Sowwah Square developments have already made good on the project's commitment to sustainability by making the area suitable for pedestrian movement and providing a walking and cycle track in a bid to reduce traffic emissions. A mass transit system is in its way and the square's design has been awarded accreditation by LEED (Leadership in Energy & Environmental Design).

Sustainable Features

The buildings of Sowwah Square are not just beautiful (note the aerofoil shape of the Rosewood hotel, it's mushroom-shaped exterior shading and the stunning steel-and-glass atrium and porch of the Galleria), they're smart too. With solar power, double-skin facades, recycled materials and active sun shading, they are designed to be energy-efficient in extreme temperatures.

☑ Top Tips

▶ Parking is an organised experience but valet parking is on offer if you're in a hurry.

▶ Taxis are available from the Galleria.

▶ Be the first at Nolu's, the highly popular American-Afghani fusion café in Abu Dhabi's outskirts, when the branch opens in 2015.

▶ The Promenade beside the square is fully lit for an evening stroll.

▶ Watch out for the Christmas market on the Promenade in December.

✗ Take a Break

Around Sowwah Square, the Rosewood hotel and the Galleria offer many fine-dining options.

For something savoury with a similar view, Bentley Bistro & Bar (p69) has already won a reputation as the place to be seen.

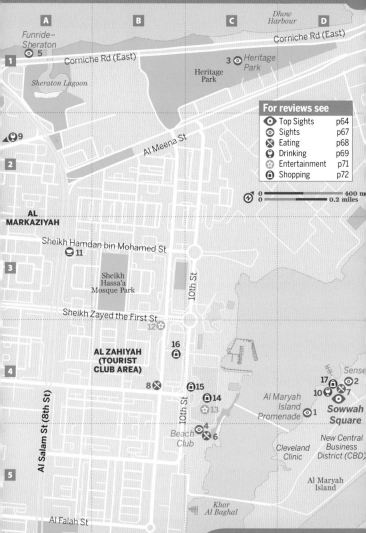

Dhow Harbour

Corniche Rd (East)

Funride–Sheraton 5

Corniche Rd (East)

Heritage Park 3 Heritage Park

Sheraton Lagoon

9

Al Meena St

For reviews see

	Top Sights	p64
	Sights	p67
	Eating	p68
	Drinking	p69
	Entertainment	p71
	Shopping	p72

0 — 400 m
0 — 0.2 miles

AL MARKAZIYAH

Sheikh Hamdan bin Mohamed St 11

Sheikh Hassa'a Mosque Park

10th St

Sheikh Zayed the First St 12

AL ZAHIYAH (TOURIST CLUB AREA)

16

Sense 17 2

8 10 7

15 Al Maryah Island Promenade 1 Sowwah Square

14

10th St 13

4 6 Beach Club

Cleveland Clinic New Central Business District (CBD)

Al Maryah Island

Al Salam St (8th St)

Khor Al Baghal

Al Falah St

IAIN MASTERTON/ALAMY ©

The Cleveland Clinic on Al Maryah Island Promenade

Sights

Al Maryah Island Promenade

PROMENADE

1 ◉ Map p66, D4

This promenade bends gently round the western shore of Al Maryah Island and offers fantastic views of Abu Dhabi and the busy channel of water in between. Used as a venue for a lavish Christmas market and New Year's fireworks, and linking an assortment of trend-setting cafes and bistros, the promenade is already a meeting place for Abu Dhabi's elite. Notable buildings along the 2km route include the upmarket Galleria, and the Cleveland Clinic that almost manages to make healthcare look inviting. (⊘24hr)

Sense

SPA

2 ◉ Map p66, D4

With nine treatment rooms, white leather lounges, and traditional hammams, this is a temple of relaxation and therapy. It offers a master class in decadent design showcasing a marble soaking tub, bronze tiles, mist rooms, fibre-optic features, and an infra-red stone wall. Soak in a Cleopatra bath with goat's milk and your tub back home will never be the same again.
(☎02-813 5537; www.rosewoodhotels.com; Rosewood Hotel; 30min milk bath Dh280; ⊘10am-11pm)

Heritage Park
PARK

3 ⊙ Map p66, C1

This attractive family park straddles both sides of the far eastern end of the Corniche, with great views of the traditional dhow harbour across the water in Al Mina. With fountains and faux grottos, barbecue facilities and play areas, it is a popular picnic site at weekends. (⏰24hr)

Local Life
Christmas in the Capital

If you think that any mention of Christmas is taboo in a Muslim country, then you may be in for a surprise! Christmas is celebrated with gusto across the Gulf, with giant faux firs in most of the malls, ho-ho-hoing Santas, nativity scenes with real goats and manufactured snow. In Abu Dhabi the following two events help spread some winter cheer:

Christmas Market (Map p66, D4; www.thegalleria.ae; Galleria, Al Maryah Island; ⏰early Dec-early Jan) Gingerbread making, craft stalls, cribs, lights and a giant tree.

Swiss Christmas Market (Map p66, C5; www.rotana.com; Beach Rotana, Al Khalidiyah; ⏰early Dec) Raclette, fondue, crafts and carols make this pre-Christmas tradition at the Beach Rotana.

Beach Club
SWIMMING

4 ⊙ Map p66, C5

With a small but pleasant beach, swimming pools and a wet bar-cafe, this club welcomes day visitors. There's an increasingly impressive view of the Al Maryah Island developments opposite. (📞02-697 9302; www.rotana.com; Beach Rotana Hotel & Towers, 10th St; s/d/child Fri & Sat Dh210/310/70, Sun-Thu Dh150/230/70; ⏰6am-11pm, pool 8am-10pm)

Funride – Sheraton
CYCLING

5 ⊙ Map p66, A1

One of the four stations along the Corniche where bikes may be hired. If this station is closed, the one outside the Hiltonia Health Club at the far southwestern end of the Corniche is more reliably staffed. (📞02-556 6113; www.funridesports.com; Corniche Rd (East); per hr adult/child Dh20/15)

Eating

Finz
SEAFOOD $$

6 🍴 Map p66, C5

Amble down the jetty and snuggle into a table at this wooden A-frame with terraces above the sea, order a cocktail and prepare for some of the finest seafood in town. Whether grilled, wok-cooked, baked or prepared in the tandoor oven, the results are invariably delicious. (📞02-697 9011; www.rotana.com; Beach Rotana Hotel & Towers, Abu Dhabi Mall; mains Dh50-100; ⏰12.30-3.30pm & 7-11.30pm)

Godiva Chocolate Café CAFE $$

7   Map p66, D4

What makes this indulgent cafe in the new Marina Mall an experience is the exceptional view of Abu Dhabi's Al Zahiyah district from the wall of windows in its mezzanine location. Beautiful cakes, pastries and chocolate-dipped strawberries are delights of the menu.
(☏02-667 0717; www.galleria.ae; Galleria Mall, Al Maryah Island; coffee & cake Dh80; ☉11am-10pm)

Automatic Restaurant LEBANESE $

8   Map p66, B4

No one has really got to the bottom of the name of this chain of unlicensed restaurants selling the local equivalent of fast food. But the name matters not, as the food (dips, grills and rocket salads) is automatically trustworthy and delicious. As Automatic Restaurants represent something of an institution across the Gulf, don't leave Abu Dhabi without at least one visit.
(☏02-677 9782; Hamdan St, Al Zahiyah; mains around Dh30; ☉8am-3pm)

Drinking

Ally Pally Corner PUB

9   off Map p66

For something low-key in a city of high-brow, the Ally Pally's infamous pub is a good place for a retro vibe – or at least reminiscent of a bygone

Top Tip

Picnic in the Park

Forget picnics back home with sandwiches, crisps and fresh fruit. A picnic local style is a sumptuous, usually nighttime affair involving barbecued meats, the extended family and portable seating. Pick up the wherewithal for your own BBQ at **Abu Dhabi Co-op Hypermarket** (Map p66, C4; ☏02-645 9777; www. abudhabicoop.com/english; ground fl, Abu Dhabi Mall, 10th St; ☉8am-midnight) and head for Heritage Park.

expat era. Quiet during the week, it metamorphoses at the weekend into the kind of venue that only solo men (or broad-minded couples) would appreciate.
(☏02-679 4777; www.alainpalacehotel.com; Al Ain Hotel; ☉noon-1am)

Bentley Bistro & Bar COCKTAIL BAR

10   Map p66, D4

With a wicked assortment of carefully crafted mocktails and cocktails, this classy bar attracts a well-dressed clientele. Balance the drinks with upper-crust snacks, such as Wagyu-beef burgers and hand-cut chips. The bistro offers a classic European menu with a suitably first-class view of Abu Dhabi's skyline.
(☏02-626 2131; www.bentleybistro.com; Galleria Mall, Al Maryah Island; mocktails/cocktails Dh30/40; ☉8am-2am)

Understand

Population & Ethnic Diversity

In Arabia, names are all important. Names tell a lot about who is from where, and each country is acutely mindful of such distinctions: 'with a name like that, he must be a Baluchi' (not real Emirati); 'he speaks Swahili so he must be Zanzibari' (not real Omani); 'he's from the coast' (not real Yemeni). And so it goes until you wonder if there's such a thing as a 'real anybody'. Such gossiping about ethnicity makes you realise that Arab allegiances are linked to tribe before nation.

Expats Outnumber Nationals

Despite this emphasis on kinship, centuries of trading and pilgrimage have resulted in a highly mixed population and only a few pockets of people, such as the Jibbalis of southern Oman – the descendants of the ancient people of Ad – can claim a single ethnic heritage. For the visitor, it is not always Arabs you'll notice anyway. In the UAE as a whole, non-nationals account for 81% of the population, making it relatively difficult to engage with the indigenous residents.

Division of Labour

The large presence of foreign nationals in the region came about after the discovery of oil. Expatriates were brought in to help develop local industries and provide skills and knowledge in creating a modern infrastructure. Western expats were originally invited to contribute specialist know-how, while those from India, Pakistan and Bangladesh supplied most of the manual labour. Filipinos joined the region's health care services and professionals from Syria, Jordan, Iraq and Egypt played an important role in education.

An Enriching Diversity

Nowadays, the distinctions of role are no longer defined to the same extent by nationality and the cosmopolitan mix continues to grow. The sense of satisfaction in being part of the rapid development of a nation, the opportunities for career development and an exciting lifestyle attract people from all over the world looking to be part of the region's dynamic future.

For a visitor this means a rich opportunity to enjoy the cuisine, shopping and cultural festivals of half a continent in the space of a single city.

Beach Club (p68) at Beach Rotana Hotel

Planet Café   SHEESHA CAFE

11   Map p66, A3

A hugely popular, independent cafe (women-friendly) that has nothing especially to write home about other than the sense of participating in a beloved local ritual. If you're keen on board games, then you'll have to be quick off the mark to reserve one. (02-676 7962; Hamdan St; mains Dh150; 8am-1.30am Sat-Thu, noon-1.30am Fri)

Entertainment

49er's The Gold Rush   LIVE MUSIC

12   Map p66, B4

This long-running nightclub has earned its spurs over the years, with its Wild West theme, cowboy hats, bucking bronco decorations, and built-in barbecue kitchen serving up Texas-sized steaks and fries. There's a resident band and DJ. (02-645 8000; www.aldiarhotels.com; Al Diar Dana Hotel, cnr Zayed the First & Al Firdous Sts; noon-3am)

Grand Cinemas
Abu Dhabi   CINEMA

13 ⭐ Map p66, C4

This multiplex shows the latest
Hollywood films, some of which are
shown in 3D.
(📞02-645 8988; www.grandcinemas.com;
Level 3, Abu Dhabi Mall; tickets Dh35)

Shopping

Abu Dhabi Mall   MALL

14 🔒 Map p66, C4

This elegant mall has the expected
200 stores, cinemas and children's
amusements, but it also has shops
with a local twist. On Level 3, head
for Arabesq sweets (from Syria,
Oman, Lebanon, Jordan, and honey
from Yemen) and the Al Rifai nut
shop. On Level 1, Bateel dates make
good gifts.

The discerning Emirati browser
will buy *ouds* (perfumes) from
Cambodia and India in the celebrated
store called Yas – The Royal Name
of Perfumes (Level 1). Also on Level
1, *abayas* (women's outer garments)
cost around Dh1700 from Khunji,
while men's delicate *bishts* (outer
garment worn on ceremonial occa-
sions) cost anything from Dh300 to
Dh2000.
(📞02-645 4858; www.abudhabi-mall.com;
10th St; 🕙10am-10pm Sat-Wed, to 11pm Thu,
4-10pm Fri)

Understand
Shopping for Souvenirs

One of the many rewards of a city with a high density of expatriates is a lively
trade between nations. This is evident at the macro level, of course, with
various departments of trade and commerce lobbying hard for favoured
status on behalf of their sovereign nations. But it's also evident at the micro
level, with many local outlets representing the goods of the local expatriate
communities.

While electrical fittings from India or ceramics tiles from Germany may
not be of much interest to the visitor, there are many goods that are. Feel
it's not authentic to buy Syrian boxes from an Indian tradesman in Abu
Dhabi? On the contrary, in buying Kashmiri pashminas or Turkish lanterns
from Keralite shop-owners you'll be participating in a pattern of trade that
has been going on locally for centuries. Here are some great buys on sale
in Al Zahiyah: painted ceramics (Turkey); wooden inlaid boxes (Syria); sand
bottles (Jordan); cotton towels (Egypt); dates (Saudi); camel-leather baskets
(Oman); *khanjas* (daggers – Yemen); carpets (Iran); embroidered shawls
(Kashmir); printed clothing (India); and spices (Sri Lanka).

Jashanmal
DEPARTMENT STORE

15 Map p66, C4

Set up by an Indian businessman in 1919 in Basra, Iraq, this wholesale and retail enterprise has become the Gulf's answer to Debenhams or Macy's. (02-644 3869; Abu Dhabi Mall; 10am-10pm Sat-Wed, to 11pm Thu, 4-10pm Fri)

Khalifa Centre
SOUVENIRS, HANDICRAFTS

16 Map p66, B4

For a wide range of souvenirs (*sheesha* pipes, camel-bone boxes, stuffed leather camels, carpets and cushion covers) head to the Khalifa Centre, across the road from the Abu Dhabi Mall, where you'll find a dozen independent stores, mostly run by the expat Indian community, selling handicrafts and carpets.

Most of the goods on sale are from India, Turkey and Syria and many are made in China, but it's a fun place to root around and try your bargaining skills.

(10th St; 10am-1pm & 4-10pm Sat-Thu, 4-10pm Fri)

Local Life
Grand Gifts from Grand Stores

Looking for a gift for someone who has everything? What about a miniature silver oil rig complete with helicopter and landing pad (Dh2315)? More modest oil platforms go for half the price. The **Grand Stores** (Map p66, C4; Abu Dhabi Mall; 10am-10pm Sat-Wed, to 11pm Thu, 4-10pm Fri) is also the place to buy a giant silver-plated falcon or a wooden dhow.

Galleria
MALL

17 Map p66, D4

One of the newest and most elegant shopping malls is being promoted as 'Abu Dhabi's foremost lifestyle destination' with valet parking, big-name designers and highly fashionable, internationally branded restaurants. (02-616 6999; www.thegalleria.ae; Al Maryah Island; 10am-10pm Sat-Wed, to midnight Thu, noon-midnight Fri)

Explore

Al Mina & Saadiyat Island

This neighbourhood casts an interesting light on Abu Dhabi's cultural inheritance, past and present, and affords a glimpse of the city's future as artistic capital of the Gulf with the Abu Dhabi Louvre. The port is home to the old dhow harbour and interesting souqs, while Saadiyat Island's sandy beaches and protected coastal environment offer a world removed from urban life.

The Sights in a Day

☀ It's never too early to browse the 24-hour markets of Al Mina, the port district. Learn about dates at the **Fruit & Vegetable Market** (p79), haggle for rugs with the Baluchis in the **Carpet Souq** (p78) and buy Gulf essentials, including rice mats and enamel bowls, in the **Iranian Souq** (p79). Stroll to the **dhow harbour** (p81) where seafarers mend nets beside traditional wooden boats.

☀ See what a night at sea fished up in the neighbouring market before sampling the catch at traditional **Al Arish** (p85), the best Emirati buffet in town. Cross the bridge to Saadiyat Island and learn about the city's rapid development from 'rags to riches' and its vision for the future in **Manarat Al Saadiyat** (p76). Catch a show at the neighbouring **UAE Pavilion** (p83), shaped like wind-blown sand dunes.

☽ Watch the sunset from **Saadiyat Public Beach** (p84), a beautiful stretch of coast in a protected environment where turtles nest. Continue the romance over dinner in the breeze-blown pavilions of **Turquoiz** (p86) or simply relax the local way with coffee and a *sheesha*.

For a local's day at the markets of Al Mina, see p78.

◉ Top Sights
Manarat Al Saadiyat (p76)

◔ Local Life
Markets of Al Mina (p78)

♥ Best of Abu Dhabi

Eating
Al Arish Restaurant (p85)

Al Mina Modern Cuisine (p79)

Beach House (p86)

Turquoiz (p86)

Architecture
Manarat Al Saadiyat (p76)

Abu Dhabi Louvre (p83)

UAE Pavilion (p83)

Beaches & Spas
Saadiyat Beach Club (p84)

Saadiyat Public Beach (p84)

Getting There

🚌 **Bus** Route 403 connects Abu Dhabi Island with Al Mina and Saadiyat Island.

🚌 **Shuttle Bus** The free Yas Express connects Saadiyat and Yas Islands.

🚌 **Big Bus** The big bus tour stops outside Manarat Al Saadiyat.

Top Sights
Manarat Al Saadiyat

For a glimpse of Abu Dhabi's expansive ambitions of the future, a visit to the 'place of enlightenment' (Manarat Al Saadiyat) is an excellent way to understand the breadth of vision involved in creating a cultural hub from scratch. The visitor centre, housed in a postmodern structure with a honeycomb mantel, holds a permanent display of architectural models showcasing the key destinations planned for the Cultural District and a contemporary gallery showing international exhibitions.

👁 Map p80, D2

📞 02-657 5800

www.saadiyat.ae

Cultural District, Saadiyat Island

admission free

🕘 9am-8pm

Manarat Al Saadiyat's contemporary gallery

Don't Miss

Rags to Riches

The permanent exhibition space inside Manarat Al Saadiyat charts the history of Abu Dhabi, from the small pearling village of *barasti* (palm-frond) houses of the 1970s to the cosmopolitan metropolis of today. A set of photographs captures the founding fathers of the UAE with their mission to create a world-class destination that encompassed and amplified local culture.

Model Cultural District

The highlight of Manarat Al Saadiyat is undoubtedly the 'Saadiyat Experience', which displays large architectural models of the Cultural District's three key building projects. Each of the models – the Abu Dhabi Louvre (due to open in 2015), Sheikh Zayed National Museum (2016) and the Guggenheim Abu Dhabi (2017) – is to scale and accompanied by slide presentations.

The Master Builders

It's worth reading the monographs of the international architects who won the contracts to build the densest cluster of world-class cultural destinations of the 21st century. Norman Foster's five-tower museum, for example, takes inspiration from the wing tips of falcons, while Frank Gehry's Guggenheim hints at ancient Emirati wind towers.

Abu Dhabi Louvre

The Abu Dhabi Louvre (p83), designed by Jean Nouvel, should be completed by the time you read this and will form one of the leading collections of fine art in the world.

☑ Top Tips

▶ Notice the design of Manarat Al Saadiyat – it's an award-winning building in its own right.

▶ The Louvre's forthcoming displays will transcend geographical boundaries and focus on cultural interconnectivity.

▶ To learn more about the Louvre concept, see the Manarat Al Saadiyat website.

▶ See What's On listings in the daily papers for visiting exhibitions (usually free).

▶ Concerts during the Abu Dhabi Classics (p58) season are often performed here.

▶ The UAE Pavilion (p83) next door also houses exhibitions.

✗ Take a Break

Stylish Fanr (p85), inside Manarat Al Saadiyat, offers the perfect place for lunch.

For snacks in a glorious beachside setting, head for Saadiyat Public Beach (p84).

Local Life
Markets of Al Mina

The souqs of the port area are rewarding to explore. They may have concrete rather than *barasti* ceilings and be air-conditioned rather than piled along dusty alleyways, but the modern market stalls here are every bit as traditional in spirit as their ancient predecessors. Visitors are welcome, as long as they don't interfere with the important business of making a sale!

❶ **A Pile of Polyester**
Forget notions of Oriental bazaars selling fine Persian silk carpets, the **Carpet Souq** (⏱9am-11pm) in Al Mina is far more authentic! This is where the average Gulf family comes to buy a washable polyester carpet for the *majlis* (meeting rooms), a new portable prayer rug or a set of cushions and floor-level settees upholstered in traditional Bedouin geometric patterns of red, black and green. The gar-

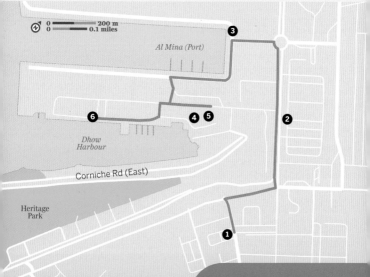

rulous traders from Baluchistan are very friendly, but don't expect to leave without at least a cushion cover!

❷ Onions Anyone?

The vast wholesale **Fruit and Vegetable Market** (⊘24hr, shops 7am-midnight), part of which is open-air, is the exchange point for melons from Jordan, potatoes from Turkey and onions from just about everywhere. The best part of a visit is cruising along 'dates alleyway' where shops sell around 45 different varieties. Giant *majdool* dates from Saudi cost Dh65 per kilo, while medicinal *ajwa* dates fetch Dh110 per kilo.

❸ All the Things You Never Knew You Wanted

If you've never been to a regional wholesale hardware market before, then the **Iranian Souq** (⊘7am-midnight), a cramped collection of stalls huddled around the harbour edge, is a fun destination. Aluminium cooking pots large enough to cook for a family of 14, brooms, ropes, melamine trays sporting European floral designs, Chinese plastic decorations, wicker-ware, thermoses and modern copper coffeepots are just some of the assorted imports in this lively souq. Look out for a few local crafts like rice mats (around Dh40).

❹ Catch of the Day

Never mind the prospect of lots of tasty seafood, the fish market is a visual feast of colour, texture and design. Rhythmical arrangements of prawns, orange-spotted trevally, blue-shelled crabs, red snappers, pink Sultan Ibrahims and a host of unlikely edibles from the sea straddle the ice bars of this large **fish market** (Dhow Harbour, Al Mina; ⊘5am-11pm).

❺ Try Something Fishy

If you really want a flavour of local life, nose round the back of the fish market, near the dry fish section. **Matam Fiyroom** (Fish Market, Al Mina; set lunch from Dh6; ⊘5am-11pm), a tiny Indian restaurant (name in Arabic only), serves as a canteen for harbour hands and traders, but they are accommodating to those looking to sample their delicious set platters of rice, fish, *sambal* and *dahl*. It's not for the faint-hearted, but it's a great place to interact with Abu Dhabi's seafarers.

❻ From Dhow to Dinner Plate

If you don't have the stomach for eating in the fish market, then head for a local alternative called **Al Mina Modern Cuisine & Restaurant** (☎02-673 3390; Al Mina; mains Dh45; ⊘noon-midnight) instead. Most visitors steam on past this wonderful little eatery in the hunt for its more famous neighbour, Al Arish Restaurant. That's a pity because the ambience here is every bit as authentic, with lots of old photographs on the wall, pet fish in the aquarium and the catch of the day delivered virtually from dhow to dinner plate. Its harbourside location makes a great place to end this neighbourhood tour.

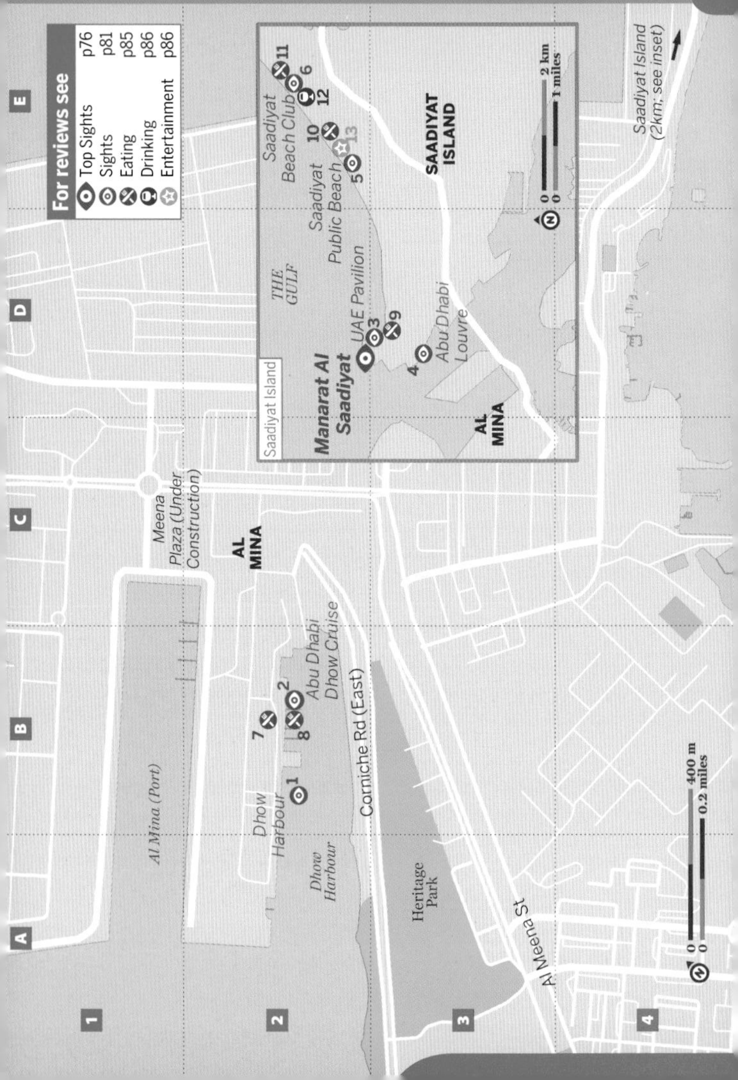

For reviews see
Top Sights p76
Sights p81
Eating p85
Drinking p86
Entertainment p86
A
B
C
D
E
1
2
3
4
Al Mina (Port)
Meena Plaza (Under Construction)
AL MINA
Dhow Harbour
Dhow Harbour
Abu Dhabi Dhow Cruise
Corniche Rd (East)
Heritage Park
Al Meena St
Saadiyat Island (2km; see inset)
1
2
7
8
0
400 m
0
0.2 miles
Saadiyat Island
Manarat Al Saadiyat
UAE Pavilion
Abu Dhabi Louvre
THE GULF
Saadiyat Public Beach
Saadiyat Beach Club
SAADIYAT ISLAND
AL MINA
3
4
5
6
9
10
11
12
13
0
2 km
0
1 miles

Traditional wooden dhows at Al Mina fish market (p78)

Sights

Dhow Harbour

HARBOUR

1 ◉ Map p80, B2

There's nothing quite so fascinating than sitting by the harbourside watching these beautiful old wooden boats slip off to sea. At any time of day there's work going on as fishermen mend their nets, pile up lobster pots, hang out colourful sarongs to dry, unload fish and congregate for communal chats about the weather. Surveying the resting dhows strung together, five abreast, Abu Dhabi's modern backdrop is almost forgotten and it's ancient past as a pearling village revealed. (Al Mina)

Abu Dhabi Dhow Cruise

CRUISE

2 ◉ Map p80, B2

This company offers lunch (1.30pm to 3pm), sunset (5.45pm to 6.45pm) and dinner (8pm to 10pm) cruises. The food is simple fare but includes fresh fish. There is a minimum of 15 required for the lunch and sunset trips, which cruise along from the harbour. For an extra fee, the company operates a pick up service from major hotels.
(☎052-214 4369; www.abudhabidhowcruise. com; Dhow Harbour, Al Mina; adult/child Dh200/100)

CHRIS MELLOR/GETTY IMAGES ©

Understand

Cultural Capital

Now that construction is near completion, there is great anticipation about the collection to be displayed inside the Abu Dhabi Louvre. Paintings from the holdings of the Paris Louvre are of course promised, but it will be interesting to see if canvases from the city hosting this major new gallery will find wall space too. There is a growing number of talented Emirati artists and their work is beginning to attract international attention; however, it is fair to say that painting is a relatively nascent genre in the region.

Portable, Practical Crafts

Crafts have traditionally been a more notable art form in the Gulf, thanks in part to a partially Bedouin heritage. The nomadic pre-oil lifestyle of part of the population dictated a life refined of excess baggage, so creativity found its most obvious expression in poetry, song, storytelling and portable, practical crafts.

In crafts such as jewellery, silversmithing, weaving, embroidery and basketry, function and form combine in artefacts that document a way of life. Take the heavy silver so distinctively worn by Bedouin women, which is designed not just as a personal adornment but as a form of portable wealth. Silver amulets contained rolled pieces of parchment or paper bearing protective inscriptions from the Quran to guarantee the safety of the wearer. These were considered useful against the perils of the evil eye – the envy or malice of others.

Reviving Local Heritage

At the end of a piece of jewellery's (or its wearer's) life, the silver was traditionally melted down and traded in as an ultimate gesture of practicality. In the same vein, it is the sad fact of practical craft that once the need for it has passed, there is little incentive to maintain the skills. Why bother with clay ewers when everyone drinks water from plastic bottles?

Aware of this, craft associations have sprung up in the hope of keeping local heritage alive. Complementing this effort, Saadiyat's Cultural District (p76) will eventually play an important part in documenting the Gulf's craft legacy.

Model of the new developments being built on Saadiyat Island

UAE Pavilion   BUILDING

3 Map p80, D3

Shaped like two parallel sand dunes, smooth and curvaceous on the windward side, steep and rippled on the eroded side, this award-winning building by British architect, Sir Norman Foster and partners, was designed for the 2010 Shanghai Expo. Now used as an exhibition space for touring cultural shows, this striking building is worth a visit in its own right. It particularly comes into its own in November when it hosts the Abu Dhabi Contemporary Art Fair.
(02-406 1501; www.saadiyatculturaldistrict.ae; Cultural District, Saadiyat Island; admission free)

Abu Dhabi Louvre   GALLERY

4 Map p80, D3

The Louvre, designed by Jean Nouvel, is well on the way to completion. Already the theme of palm tree shading is detectable in the elaborate filigree domed roof which seems to hover over the structure, and which will create a rain of light in the interior. Rumoured to open at the end of 2015, the Louvre will form one of the leading collections of fine art (objects and paintings) in the world with loans from French museums.

If you want to know more about the concept of the collection, there is a good website which explains the unique approach to displays that will transcend geographical boundaries and focus on cultural interconnectivity. While the gallery is still under construction, it's worth calling into the 'Saadiyat Experience' in Manarat Al Saadiyat (p77) where you can see a full-scale model of the Louvre and interesting accounts of the inspiration behind its unique design. (www.saadiyat.ae; Cultural District, Saadiyat Island)

Saadiyat Public Beach

WATERSPORTS

5 Map p80, E2

A boardwalk leads through a protected zone of coastal vegetation to this beautiful powdery white beach,

home to nesting turtles, on the north-west coast of Saadiyat Island. There's a lifeguard during daylight hours and towels are available for Dh10. Also for rent are kayaks (Dh80/hr), skimboards (Dh50/hr), paddle boats (Dh120/hr) and body boards (Dh50/hr). The club is unlicensed. (BAKE Beach; www.bakeuae.com; Saadiyat Island; adult/child Dh25/15; 8am-sunset)

Saadiyat Beach Club

SPA

6 Map p80, E2

This luxurious and exclusive beach club, spa and fitness centre is open to day visitors and offers a full spa experience, beautiful pools and an expanse of pristine beach. Protected Hawksbill

Saadiyat Beach Club

sea turtles nest along this coast and the occasional school of dolphins is spotted in the turquoise waters. (📞02-656 3500; www.saadiyatbeachclub. ae; Saadiyat Island; weekend day rate couple/ adult/child Dh525/315/free; 🕙beach 9am-sunset, other facilities to 8pm)

Eating

Al Arish Restaurant MIDDLE EASTERN $$

 Map p80, B2

This aged, flamboyant gem, with its fading Arabian decor, *barasti* ceiling and hand-carved furniture, sports a sumptuous *majlis* (lounge) that has entertained princes and sheikhs over the decades despite the unlikely harbourside venue. The lunch buffet offers one of the best opportunities in Abu Dhabi to sample local dishes, including *ouzi* (baked lamb) and *majboos* (chicken baked in rice).

Al Arish supplies the buffet for the popular Al Dhafra evening dinner cruise. (📞673 2266; Al Mina; lunch & dinner buffet Dh175; 🕙noon-4.30pm & 7pm-midnight)

Al Dhafra BUFFET, EMIRATI $$$

8 Map p80, B2

This floating restaurant is on board a traditional dhow. The popular Al Arish Restaurant supplies the buffet for the nightly dinner cruise from Al Mina to the Breakwater and back. Al Dhafra offers a fun setting,

Top Tip

DIY Fish Supper

For a memorable meal for under Dh20, buy fresh prawns at the fish market (Map p80, B2) from the men in blue, then take them to the men in red at the gutting and filleting station. Take the fillets next door (alongside the dry fish section) and jostle with seafarers for your favourite spices. Beyond the spice area, give your purchases to the cooks who will turn them into a fiery hot curry or grill them rubbed in salt and dried chillies. Take the finished dish to the dhow harbour outside and sit on a lobster pot to eat it!

while sitting cross-legged on sedans and cushions on deck, for sampling Emirati dishes with stunning views of Abu Dhabi's night-time skyline for entertainment. (📞02-673 2266; Dhow Harbour, Al Mina; dinner cruise per person Dh180; 🕙cruise 8-10pm)

Fanr Restaurant INTERNATIONAL $$

9 Map p80, D3

This sophisticated casual dining restaurant, with floor-to-ceiling windows, and dressed in shades of white like the exhibition space that surrounds it, offers some imaginative salads, smoothies, and regional and international favourites. (📞02-657 5888; www.fanrrestaurant.ae; Manarat Al Saadiyat, Saadiyat Island; mains Dh55; 🕙10am-11pm)

Turquoiz
SEAFOOD **$$**

10 Map p80, E2

It would be hard to find a more romantic venue for a sunset drink, a bowl of mussels and an ambient waft of *sheesha*. Housed in a set of wooden pavilions with decked terraces overlooking the sea, this lovely restaurant feels a world away from the pseudo-Mediterranean hotel to which it belongs, let alone the city beyond. (☏02-498 8888; www.turquoizabudhabi.com; St Regis Saadiyat Island Resort; mains from Dh50; ☺noon-3pm & 6.30-11pm)

Beach House
MEDITERRANEAN **$$**

11 Map p80, E2

Open for breakfast, lunch and dinner, this restaurant, with its emphasis on

homely cooked Mediterranean fare, has an enviable location amid the sand dunes on the Saadiyat Island coast. In the cooler months, go up to the Beach House Rooftop (5pm to 1am) for arguably the best views of the sunset in Abu Dhabi. (☏02-407 1138; http://abudhabi.park.hyatt.com; Park Hyatt Abu Dhabi; mains from Dh60; ☺9am-midnight)

Drinking

De La Costa
LOUNGE

12 Map p80, E2

With a beautiful vista, comfortable armchairs and sophisticated tipples, this is a delightful place to watch the sun go down across the water. (☏02-656 3572; Saadiyat Beach Club; ☺4pm-midnight Sat-Wed, to 2am Thu & Fri)

Entertainment

People by Crystal Abu Dhabi
LIVE PERFORMANCE

13 Map p80, E2

Offering what the promoters describe as a 'mash up of house and urban music', this superchic nightclub brings international artists, theatrical and musical extravaganzas and high-tech projections on the sophisticated LED screens. Needless to say, it attracts Abu Dhabi's elite and delivers on its promise of a serious night out. (☏050-297 2097; St Regis Saadiyat Island Resort; ☺11pm-4am Thu & Fri)

Local Life

Women's Handicraft Centre

This government-run **handicraft centre** (☏02-447 6645; Al Karamah/24th St; admission Dh5; ☺7am-3pm Sun-Thu) showcases textile weaving, embroidery, basketry, silver-thread needlework and other time-honoured crafts traditional to the region. Shoes should be removed before entering the workshops and permission sought for photographs. All items are for sale in the on-site shop, which lies a little outside the neighbourhoods covered here, in the heart of the city's suburbs.

Understand
Eating Etiquette

If you find yourself cross-legged on the timbers of a dhow with a communal plate in front of you, it's good to know a few tips about local protocol. Here are some of the main things to think about when dining the traditional Arab way:

▶ It's polite to be seen washing your hands before eating.

▶ It's considered rude to eat with your legs stretched out.

▶ Don't take the best parts of the meat – if you're a guest, your host will be sure to lavish them on you.

▶ Strictly use only your right hand (the left hand is reserved for ablutions) for eating or passing food.

▶ Discard unwanted food in a napkin rather than returning it to the communal plate.

▶ Leave a little food on your plate to avoid inviting famine.

▶ Feel free to pick your teeth after dinner.

▶ Don't leave the meal before coffee is served...

▶ ...but don't stay for too long afterwards. Most of the chatting is done before dinner, less during and almost none after!

Explore

Sheikh Zayed Grand Mosque & Around

Three bridges straddle the approach from the mainland to Abu Dhabi Island, and from each there is one sight that crowns the view: the Sheikh Zayed Grand Mosque. This exquisite building is not just an exceptional piece of architecture, it also represents the living soul of this heritage-minded Emirate. Nearby attractions include the worthwhile new developments of Bain Al Jessrain.

The Sights in a Day

☼ The magnificent **Sheikh Zayed Grand Mosque** (p90) is the focus of the day's itinerary and it's never far from view. Take the 90-minute free tour in the morning (except Friday) and visit the **library** (p93). Inspired by the mosque's beauty, travel along to **Miraj Islamic Centre** (p93), a collection of regional fine arts. Head over (and then under) Al Maqta Bridge to photograph **Maqta Fort** (p95); lost in the suburbs, this fort and its watchtower in the *khor* (coastal inlet) are important parts of the city's heritage.

☼ Head to the water's edge and brunch at **Giornotte** (p101) on Fridays; on other days, **Ushna** (p99) offers locally loved Indian cuisine with views of the mosque. Stroll the promenade and visit the boutique shops of **Souq Qaryat al Beri** (p101).

☾ Pick up the pace at the world-class bowling alley at **Zayed Sports City** (p97) and then take an angle on dinner – 18° to be precise – in **Capital Gate** (p96), the world's most leaning building. Finish the evening at **Cooper's** (p99), a favourite watering hole with popular ladies' nights.

 Top Sights

Sheikh Zayed Grand Mosque (p90)

♥ **Best of Abu Dhabi**

Eating
18° (p98)

Mijana (p98)

Giornotte (p101)

Ushna (p99)

Entertainment
Chameleon (p101)

Giornotte (p101)

Shopping
Souq Qaryat al Beri (p101)

Getting There

🚌 **Bus** The 032 route links Sports City with Al Maqta.

🚕 **Taxi** Offers the most convenient way of getting to the resorts either side of the *khor* in Bain Al Jessrain.

🚌 **Big Bus** This hop-on, hop-off tour bus stops right outside Sheikh Zayed Grand Mosque and continues on to the Eastern Corniche.

Top Sights
Sheikh Zayed Grand Mosque

Rising majestically from beautifully manicured gardens and visible from each of the bridges joining Abu Dhabi Island to the mainland, the Sheikh Zayed Grand Mosque represents an impressive welcome to the city. Conceived by the first president of the UAE, Sheikh Zayed, and marking his final resting place, the mosque accommodates 41,000 worshippers and is one of few regional mosques open to visitors. If the exterior is a wondrous sight, the interior is inspirational – a masterpiece of contemporary art and design.

👁 Map p18

📞 02-441 6444

www.szgmc.ae

2nd Sheikh Rashid bin Saeed al Maktoum St

admission free

🕐 9am-10pm Sat-Thu, 4.30-11pm Fri

Sheikh Zayed Grand Mosque interior

Don't Miss

The Marble Exterior
With more than 80 marble domes dancing on a roofline held aloft by over 1000 pillars and punctuated by four 107m-high minarets, Sheikh Zayed Grand Mosque is a masterpiece of modern Islamic architecture. Delicate floral designs inlaid with semi-precious stones, such as lapis lazuli, agate, amethyst and mother-of-pearl, contrast with more traditional geometric ceramic details.

Contemporary Interior
While including references to traditional Mamluk, Ottoman and Fatimid styles, the overwhelming impression of the breathtaking interior is contemporary and innovative, with three steel, gold, brass and crystal chandeliers filling the main prayer hall with shafts of primary coloured light. The chandeliers, the largest of which weighs approximately 12 tons, sparkle with Swarovski crystals and shine with 40 kilos of 24kt galvanised gold.

Hand-Loomed Carpet
One of the prayer hall's most impressive features is the world's largest loomed carpet (p100). The medallion design with elaborate arabesque motifs took 1200 craftsmen two years to complete, half of which was spent on hand knotting the 5700 square metres of woollen thread on a cotton base. That translates to 2.268 billion knots!

Lighting the Night
Over 100,000 tons of pure white Greek and Macedonian marble was used in the construction of the mosque, cleverly illuminated at night to reflect the phases of the moon. Dark clouds are projected onto the exterior during the crescent moon, while increasingly brilliant light is used during the full moon.

☑ Top Tips

▶ Free 45- to 60-minute guided tours (in English) begin at 10am, 11am and 5pm, Sunday to Thursday, with an extra tour at 2pm on Saturday. Tours are at 5pm and 7pm on Friday.

▶ Visitors can enter by themselves except during prayer times.

▶ All visitors must wear long, loose-fitting, ankle-length trousers or skirts, long sleeves and a headscarf for women.

▶ Women may loan *abeyyas* with hoods for free from the basement.

▶ Photographs are permitted; inappropriate selfies are not.

▶ Sheikh Zayed's mausoleum is on the approach to the mosque entrance. Prayers are continually recited by attendants (no photographs).

✗ Take a Break

Nearby Mijana (p98) serves contemporary twists on traditional Arabian themes.

E22

Al Maqta
Park

Sas an
Nakhi
Island

Petroleum
Institute

**AL
MAQTA**

Al Maqta Fort &
Watchtower

Sheikh
Zayed
Bridge

22
16
13
18

Khor al
Maqta

Khor Al
Maqta

Umm Al Nar
Power Station

3
20
14
4

5

15
21

**ABU DHABI
GATE CITY**

Sheikh Zayed Grand
Mosque Centre Library

1

Musafah Bridge

Eastern Corniche and
Eastern Mangroves (3km)

9 B

Sheikh Zayed St

Byky Bike 10 8
Abu
Dhabi
Murjan Tourist Authority
Splash Park

7 17

Khalifa Park

Khalifa
Park

Al Bateen
Executive
Airport

**Sheikh Zayed
Grand Mosque**

1

Al Khaleel Al Arabi St

**OFFICERS
CLUB**

Rashid bin Saeed
al Maktoum St

Al Khaleel Al Arabi St

Miraj
Islamic
Centre 2

Old
Airport
Park

**ZAYED
SPORTS
CITY**

Zayed
Sports
City

11

6
12
19

1 km
0.5 miles

N

For reviews see

⊙	Top Sights	p90
⊙	Sights	p93
✕	Eating	p98
🍷	Drinking	p99
✪	Entertainment	p101
🛍	Shopping	p101

TONY BURNS/GETTY IMAGES ©

Sheikh Zayed Bridge (p95)

Sights

Sheikh Zayed Grand Mosque Centre Library LIBRARY

1 ◉ Map p92, C3

With rare collections of Arabic calligraphy and copies of the Quran dating back to the 16th century, this priceless collection of manuscripts is intended primarily as a research centre but is also open to public view. Part of the magic of the collection is its location in the mosque's minaret, giving an aerial perspective on the mosque's magnificent multiple domes and the city and outlying islands beyond. (☎02-441 6444; www.szgmc.ae; 4th fl, North Minaret, Sheikh Zayed Grand Mosque; admission free; ☽9.30am-4.30pm Sat, 9am-8pm Sun-Wed, to 4pm Thu)

Miraj Islamic Centre MUSEUM

2 ◉ Map p92, A2

Showcasing beautiful objects from around the Islamic world, including Persian carpets, calligraphy, ceramics and textiles, this private, museum-quality collection is open for view, with some pieces also for sale. There is a second showroom in the south-facing villas (Villa 14b) on the Breakwater, near Marina Mall. (☎02-650 5830; www.mirajabudhabi.com; Rashid bin Saeed al Maktoum St, ground fl, Hilton Abu Dhabi Capital Grand; admission free; ☽9am-7pm)

Understand
The Religion of Islam

One of the most memorable sensations of a visit to Abu Dhabi, especially for visitors new to the Arab world, is likely to be the haunting sound at dawn and dusk of the call to prayer. Although the chants of the *imam* (spiritual leader) echo around the city five times a day, it is at sunrise and sunset that the 'music' of the mosque is at its most affecting.

Islam in the UAE
Muslims account for around 96% of the UAE's population. Unlike in countries where the sacred and the secular are rigorously separated, in the Arabian Peninsula religion informs all aspects of life, including culture, society and law. Recognising the integrity of religion and life makes sense of certain customs a visitor to the capital city may encounter and in turn helps guide appropriate conduct.

The Five Pillars of Islam
There are five articles of faith that must be upheld by Muslims:

Shahada Muslims must proclaim the following: 'There is no God but Allah and Mohammed is his Prophet.'

Salat Five times a day (at sunrise, noon, mid-afternoon, sunset and at night) Muslims must pray – in a mosque if possible, but on a prayer mat by the roadside will do.

Zakat This is the duty of alms giving. Muslims are expected to give a portion of their salary to those in need.

Ramadan It was during the month of Ramadan that Mohammed received his first revelation in AD 610. Muslims mark this special event each year by fasting from sunrise until sunset through the holy month.

Hajj Every Muslim capable of doing so is expected to perform the hajj pilgrimage to Mecca, the holiest city in Islam, at least once in his or her lifetime. Muslims believe that the reward for performing hajj is forgiveness of all past sins.

The Quran
The Quran is understood to be the literal word of God, unlike the Bible or Torah, which Muslims believe were inspired by God but were recorded subject to human interpretation.

Al Maqta Fort & Watchtower

FORT

3 Map p92, D2

Despite being one of the oldest sights in Abu Dhabi, this 200-year-old guardian of the city was restored and then more or less abandoned. The tourist information centre once housed there is also now closed. Although neglected, this old relic, with its companion watchtower on a rocky island in Khor al Maqta (the so-called Abu Dhabi Grand Canal), is worth an up-close view – if you can find it!

There are lots of brown signs leading to the fort, but it is frustratingly difficult to get to. Take the road into Al Maqta district, turn sharp right at the first roundabout and follow the road leading under Al Maqta Bridge (an icon of the 1960s) to the fort, which is marooned in the middle of highways and building sites.
(Al Maqta Bridge; admission free; ⏱24hr, interior closed)

Khor al Maqta

WATERFRONT

4 Map p92, D2

This historic waterway separates Abu Dhabi from the mainland, guarded by the now-somewhat hidden Al Maqta Fort and a small watchtower, on a rocky promontory in the middle of the *khor*. Referred to by some as the 'Grand Canal', both sides of the *khor* have been developed as a luxury resort destination and the charming Souq Qaryat al Beri.

Walking paths and *abras* (small traditional water taxis) help visitors move between one attraction and the next. On the immediate horizon, Sheikh Zayed Grand Mosque graces the view, a beacon toward the city beyond.
(Bain Al Jessrain)

Sheikh Zayed Bridge

BRIDGE

5 Map p92, D2

Said to symbolise the flow of energy into the capital, this stunning modern bridge designed by Zaha Hadid is reputedly the most intricate bridge in the world. Its curvilinear form is reminiscent of sand dunes and at night the lighting scheme gives a sense that the dunes are on the move.

☑ Top Tip

Water Taxi Service

Traditional wooden **water taxis** (to Eastern Mangroves one-way/return adult Dh50/80, child Dh30/50; ⏱6pm-midnight), called *abras,* ply the waters of Khor al Maqta, ferrying passengers for free from one five-star hotel to another and connecting with Souq Qaryat al Beri. In addition, the service now links this area with the hotel at the Eastern Mangroves, stopping at the Eastern Corniche on the way. This new service, which runs once an hour and takes 25 minutes one-way, offers some of the best nighttime views of Abu Dhabi.

Capital Gate

BUILDING

6 Map p92, A3

Look out of the window from many points in Abu Dhabi at night and you could be forgiven for thinking you've had one too many at the bar: the city's southeastern skyline is dominated by the odd sight of a dramatically listing skyscraper, all 35 floors of it. It's in the *Guinness Book of Records* as the world's most leaning building (at 18° westwards, it's over four times more wayward than the leaning tower of Pisa). (☏02-596 1234; http://abudhabi.capitalgate.hyatt.com; Al Khaleej al Arabi St, ADNEC)

Khalifa Park

PARK

7 Map p92, B2

This large and leafy park, not far from the Sheikh Zayed Grand Mosque, has a number of attractions including a football playing area, fountains, ponds and waterfalls, lots of shaded seating, a

⊙ Local Life

Abu Dhabi Pearl Journey

Learn more about Abu Dhabi's pearling past on board *Jalboot*, a traditional dhow. The **Pearl Journey** (☏02-641 9914; www.adpearljourney.com; Eastern Mangroves Hotel & Spa, Sheikh Zayed Rd; 90min cruise adult/child Dh500/400; ⊙cruises 9am-8pm) leaves when full (18 passengers) and includes seafaring songs, coffee, dates, oyster-opening and the chance to keep the pearl!

children's amusement park and a small train that trundles around the site. (www.adm.gov.ae; Al Salam St; adult/child Dh1/free; ⊙8am-10pm Sun-Wed, to 11pm Thu-Sat)

Eastern Corniche

PROMENADE

The seaward side of Sheikh Zayed St has been developed into a promenade to rival the main Corniche, with a series of landscaped gardens, parking bays, picnic areas and pathways. Offering excellent views of the mangroves, this is a good place to watch birds or dangle a line in the water. It gets busy on winter nights. (New Corniche; Sheikh Zayed St)

Murjan Splash Park

WATER PARK

8 Map p92, B1

Offering a range of children's activities including water slides, water guns, 'lazy river ride', trampolines and a 'surf wrangler' for learning surfing with an instructor present. (☏050-878 1009; www.murjansplashpark.weebly.com; Khalifa Park, Al Salam St; over/under 75cm Dh40/free; ⊙2-6pm & 7-11pm)

Anantara Spa

SPA

9 Map p92, B1

With 15 treatment rooms and facilities for couples, the best part of this spa is the traditional Turkish hammam. A celebration of marble, mirrors and water features, the spa feels fit for royalty. (☏02-656 1146; www.abu-dhabi.anantara.com; Eastern Mangroves Hotel; 90min signature massage Dh765; ⊙10am-10pm)

SYLVAIN SONNET/GETTY IMAGES ©

Capital Gate, designed by RMJM

Byky Bike

CYCLING

10 ◉ Map p92, B1

If you fancy a day in the saddle, Byky offers a selection of different people-powered vehicles from go-karts and bikes for four, to single-seater Ferrari-licenced pedal-powered karts. They have a popular station in Khalifa Park and also three outlets on the Corniche; the most reliably staffed is next to the Hiltonia Beach Club. Open October to April.
(📞50-844 0556; www.q8byky.com; Khalifa Park, Sheikh Zayed St; per 30min Dh20)

Zayed Sports City

BOWLING

11 ◉ Map p92, A2

Housing the Khalifa International Bowling Centre, this huge complex is open to the public; there are a somewhat intimidating 40 lanes of play. Also on-site is an ice rink and professional tennis courts, venue of the **Mubadala World Tennis Championship** (www.mubadalawtc.com), where you can play on the same court as your idol – though sadly not at the same time!
(📞02-403 4648; www.zsc.ae; Al Khaleej al Arabi St; per game from Dh15; ⊘9am-1am)

Eating

18°
MEDITERRANEAN **$$$**

12 Map p92, A3

Named after the degree of 'lean' in Abu Dhabi's famous Capital Gate skyscraper (p96), and after the 18th floor on which it's situated, this Mediterranean-style restaurant offers many Levantine favourites. Watch your dinner being cooked at the three interactive show kitchens or sit outside on the terrace and wonder how it is that food stays on the plate in this apparently leaning tower.
(02-596 1440; www.abudhabi.capitalgate. hyatt.com; Hyatt Capital Gate, Al Khaleej al Arabi St; mains from Dh120; 7-11.30pm, Fri brunch noon-3pm)

Bord Eau
FRENCH **$$$**

13 Map p92, D3

Bord Eau is *le* restaurant for French fine dining in Abu Dhabi. The classic French fare (onion soup, foie gras, chateaubriand) is flawlessly executed with a modern twist and the flavours are calibrated to perfection. With simple elegance (including reproduction Degas ballerinas gracing the walls), the ambience matches the refined quality of the food at this award-winning restaurant.
(02-509 8888; www.shangri-la.com; Shangri-La Hotel, Souq Qaryat al Beri; mains Dh90-150, five-course blind tasting menu with wine Dh500; 6.30-11.30pm)

Marco Pierre White Steakhouse & Grill
STEAK **$$$**

14 Map p92, D2

Strictly carnivore in emphasis, this restaurant is the creation of British celebrity chef Marco Pierre White. A dramatic 'flame wall' gives the dining area a Dante-esque quality, but fortunately the culinary pyrotechnics produce heavenly results. The focus is squarely on quality cuts, prepared in both classic English style and innovative grilled variations.
(02-654 3333; Fairmont Bab Al Bhar; meals around Dh250; 7.30pm-midnight)

Mijana
LEBANESE **$$**

15 Map p92, C3

Offering contemporary Lebanese cuisine with interesting twists on favourite themes, such as beetroot *moutabel* (smoked aubergine dip), six varieties of hummus and *habra niyah* (raw mince lamb 'cooked' in fresh mint and garlic). Leave space for a

---

Local Life

Café Arabia

This homely **cafe** (02-643 9699; Villa No 224/1, 15th St , between Airport (2nd) Rd & Al Karamah (24th) St; lunch around Dh 90; 8am-10pm Thu & Fri, to 11.30pm Sat-Wed), housed in a three-floor villa, is run by a Lebanese arts enthusiast. Tasty pastries and wholesome lunches are on offer but many come for the Arabian ambience.

JOCHEN TACK/ALAMY ©

Shangri-La Hotel in Qaryat Al Beri

camel's-milk smoothie or a signature-flavoured *sheesha* on the terrace with live Arabic music.
(02-818 8282; www.ritzcarlton.com; Ritz Carlton, Abu Dhabi Grand Canal; mains from Dh80; ⊙4pm-1am)

Ushna   INDIAN $$$

16 Map p92, D3

The large Indian expat community helped to construct the modern shape of Abu Dhabi and they brought with them a cuisine that is now firmly established as a local favourite. There are many local curry houses across town but this restaurant offers some of the most refined flavours, with beautiful views across the capital's 'Grand Canal' to the Sheikh Zayed Grand Mosque.
(☎02-558 1769; Souq Qaryat al Beri, Bain Al Jessrain; meals Dh250)

Drinking

Cooper's   BAR

17 Map p92, B2

A well-established bar, with an old-fashioned, wood-panelled, brass-trimmed ambience, this watering hole is renowned for its popular ladies' nights (Monday to Friday) with complimentary spirits.
(☎02-657 3333; www.rotana.com; Park Rotana Abu Dhabi; ⊙noon-2.30am)

Eight

BAR, CLUB

 18 Map p92, D4

Popular with cabin crews, this libation station at the Shangri-La delivers a potent cocktail of style. At night it morphs into a hot-stepping club that on occasion gets some really peppery DJs from the international circuit to hit the turntables. Great views. (☏02-558 1988; Shangri-La Hotel, Souq Qaryat al Beri; ☉8pm-4am)

Relax@12

BAR

19 Map p92, A3

This stylish rooftop bar indeed puts you in a mood for relaxing with mellow sounds, comfy seating and an extensive drinks menu that won't eviscerate your wallet. Sushi and tapas are available to help you stay stable and dancing in the attached **Club So-HI** (Mondays to Fridays). (☏02-654 5183; www.relaxat12.com; Khaleej al Arabi St, near ADNEC, Aloft Abu Dhabi; ☉5pm-2am Sun-Wed, to 3am Thu-Sat)

Understand
Oriental Carpets

A highlight of Sheikh Zayed Grand Mosque is the largest hand-knotted carpet in the world. For those new to Oriental floor coverings, here's a quick crammer.

What is an Oriental carpet? Designed to be walked on, even if they end up on the wall, Oriental carpets are generally handmade in a broad region stretching from Turkey to China.

Carpet or kilim? Carpets are knotted and have a pile of wool, cotton or silk; *kilims* are usually woollen and are woven and smooth.

How are carpets made? On looms with vertical and horizontal threads forming a grid. Threads are knotted onto this grid to form the pile.

What is a tribal rug? Geometric shapes are favoured in tribal carpets and *kilims*, usually produced by small communities. Elaborate curvilinear designs featuring arabesques, flowers or pictorial scenes are produced in urban workshops.

So tribal rugs are less valuable? Not necessarily. Carpets are judged by the harmony of the colour and design as much as on the density of knots or the quality of the materials used.

Entertainment

Chameleon   MIXOLOGY

20 ⭐ Map p92, D2

Cool cucumber mojitos, flaming rosemary gimlets, and Smitten Watermelon Ritas are just some of the signature cocktails shaken but not stirred by the entertaining mixologists in this sophisticated lounge bar. A resident DJ adds to the fun from 10pm onwards. (📞02-654 3333; www.fairmont.com; Fairmont Bab al Bahr, Bain Al Jessrain; cocktails around Dh50; ⏰6pm-1am)

Giornotte   LIVE MUSIC

21 ⭐ Map p92, D3

Live piano music provides the entertainment for one of the city's best brunches. If that isn't entertainment enough, there are 27 live stations (chefs preparing food at counters in the restaurant), Wagyu beef carving, a noodle-making show and oyster-opening, not to mention trips to a dedicated dessert room. For those who can resist the desire to sleep, a DJ takes the party into the Sorso Bar until the small hours. (📞02-818 8282; www.ritzcarlton.com; Ritz-Carlton Grand Canal; Friday brunch with/without drinks Dh375/275; ⏰12.30-4pm Fri)

Shopping

Souq Qaryat al Beri   SOUQ

22 Map p92, D3

This 21st-century take on the classic souq gets thumbs up for its appealing Arabian architecture and waterfront location. The shops cater to a very different clientele found at an authentic souq but many of the items on sale have their roots in Arabia, including exotic perfumes, chocolate-covered dates and hand-crafted jewellery. Some small stalls sell souvenirs and craft items. Next to the Shangri-La Hotel, between Maqta and Mussafah Bridges.

Abras help transport shoppers from one part of this waterfront complex to another. (📞02-558 1670; ⏰10am-10pm)

Explore

Yas Island & Around

Helping to define Abu Dhabi as a dynamic destination, Yas Island has blossomed into the activities hub of the capital. While the Grand Prix attracts a global audience in November, thrill-seekers visit year-round for Ferrari World's rides and simulations. As a rewarding contrast, a number of ecofriendly adventures are available in the mangrove stands dotting the edge of the beautiful Arabian Gulf.

The Sights in a Day

☼ Thrill-seekers should follow Day 4 of the Abu Dhabi Day Planner (p15). This itinerary reveals a more leisurely engagement with the island's attractions. Devote the morning to a tour of **Yas Marina Circuit** (p104) from Yas Central and picture the roar of the crowds during Grand Prix or book an up-close view from the passenger seat of an Aston Martin driven by experts.

☼ Stroll around Yas Marina, not-forgetting the local **market** (p109) on Saturday, and watch the fish in the clear marina waters. Call into **Aquarium** (p113), with its walls of water, for lunch – the fish on the menu are thankfully caught elsewhere. Relax for the afternoon on a sunbed at **Yas Beach** (p109) before paddling out to the mangroves at sunset on an **eco-tour** (p109).

☾ Continue the relaxation of the afternoon by watching the sun set over the marina, with a sundowner at **Iris** (p115). For a nightcap, move on to **Stills Bar & Brasserie** (p116) for some live music while propped up against the longest bar in Abu Dhabi.

For a local's day out exploring Yas Island, see p108.

 Top Sights

Yas Marina Circuit (p104)

Masdar City (p106)

 Local Life

The Gentler Side of Yas (p108)

♥ **Best of Abu Dhabi**

Adrenalin Rush

Yas Central (p104)

Ferrari World (p111)

Yas Waterworld (p112)

Entertainment

Burlesque (p116)

O1NE (p117)

Du Arena (p116)

Vox Cinemas (p117)

Getting There

🚌 **Yas Express** Free shuttle connecting the main attractions of Yas Island with Saadiyat Island.

🚌 **Bus** No 170 connects Yas hotels with the airport. No 180 connects Yas hotels with Al Markaziyah. No 190 connects Ferrari World with Al Markaziyah.

🚌 **Big Bus Shuttle** Offers an audio-guided route around Yas, leaving from Saadiyat Island. It includes a visit to Masdar City.

Top Sights
Yas Marina Circuit

While the circuit explodes to life each November during the Abu Dhabi Grand Prix, it's actually an interesting place to explore at any time of year. Visitors can go behind the scenes on a tour with stops at the support pit garages, the media centre and the paddock area. The setting alone, running through the heart of the extraordinary Yas Viceroy hotel and next to a vibrant marina, make it well worth a visit.

👁 Map p110, C3

📞 02-659 9800

www.yasmarinacircuit.ae

tours Dh120

🕐 tours 10am-noon & 2-4pm Tue-Sat

Yas Marina Circuit

Don't Miss

F1 Abu Dhabi Grand Prix

The circuit revs into action every November when the Formula One circus comes to town. This major event, attracting visitors from across the region as well as international racing fans, shows this spectacular circuit – one of the best in the racing calendar – to its best advantage, especially as the twilight race passes through the middle of Yas Viceroy hotel with its spectacular mantle of lights.

Circuit Tours

Except during the Grand Prix, it is possible to tour the circuit, which is a great opportunity to see behind the scenes of one of the world's most glamorous car races. Tours, in air-conditioned vehicles, can be arranged through Yas Central, the commercial hub of Yas Marina Circuit. They stop at the North Grandstand, the Yas Marina, Shams Tower and the Yas Drag Racing strip and provide insight into the high-tech facilities needed to support an event of this magnitude.

Driving in the Fast Lane

Outside of the racing calendar, **Yas Central** (☏02-659 9800; driver/passenger rides from Dh1700/500; ⏰9am-11pm) offers several opportunities to experience the Yas Marina Circuit up close – so close, in fact, that there seems to be only a friction burn between you and the race track. You can opt to drive a racing car on your own, book three laps in the passenger seat or bring your own car on a drag night.

Bookings need to be made a week in advance, either online or by phone.

☑ Top Tips

▶ Held for the first time in 2009, the Abu Dhabi Grand Prix is the last race of the Formula One season.

▶ Tours visit race control, the unique air-conditioned support pit garages, the 500-seat media centre and the paddocks.

▶ You can drive and cycle on the circuit in various guided and solo experiences.

▶ Bookings for all circuit experiences need to be made a week in advance.

✖ Take a Break

The circuit runs alongside an oasis of waterholes and delicious dining.

For a lunchtime view of the grandstands, the terrace of Cipriani (p115) is perfect. Or spend the evening at the Burlesque Restaurant & Lounge (p116), which has cabarets on Friday.

Top Sights
Masdar City

Part of a pioneering environmentally friendly community, Masdar City residents pride themselves on their green credentials. The city is open to formal visits, arranged through the Masdar City website, as well as to the casually curious who need to see it to believe it.

👁 Map p110, C5

☎ toll free 800 627 327

www.masdar.ae

btwn Hwys E10 & E20, just west of the airport

🕐 8.30am-4.30pm Sun-Thu

An electric car at the Masdar Institute of Science and Technology

Don't Miss

Minimising the Effects of Urbanisation

Cities occupy around 2% of the world's landmass but demand 80% of the world's resources and are responsible for 75% of its carbon emissions. The eco-project at Masdar City is conducting pioneering work into ways of minimising the negative environmental impact of this increasing urbanisation through solar and other green technologies.

Pioneering Research

Masdar City is built around a research hub, the Masdar Institute of Science and Technology. This graduate university initiates various innovative projects that explore sustainable technologies for energy production, desalination and water conservation. Research interests include electricity-driven transportation, energy-saving building techniques and the development of greener building materials.

Practising as Preached

The community, which is one day expected to house 40,000 residents and attract an additional 50,000 commuters, live in a tailor-made green environment. As you tour the complex, notice the 45m wind tower that channels cooler air to the courtyard below, solar panels on the Knowledge Centre and reflective building facades that minimise heat transfer. The city encompasses one of the largest solar plants in the Middle East.

☑ Top Tips

▶ Download the City Tour Map from the website for a 90-minute walking route.

▶ Ride (at 40km/h) on the 24-hour, electric-powered, driverless Personal Rapid Transit (PRT) system.

▶ Sign a digital guest book for a unique, computer-generated legacy of your visit.

✕ Take a Break

Assemble an organic picnic from the **Organic Foods and Café** (☎02-557 1406; www.organicfoods andcafe.com; Masdar City; sandwiches from Dh30; ⏱9.30am-7pm Sat-Thu), choose a bento box or have lunch at one of the Masdar community restaurants.

Nearby Nolu's (p108) is an American restaurant with an Afghani twist.

Local Life
The Gentler Side of Yas

Yas Island has a deserved reputation as a thrill-seeker's paradise, with Ferrari World, Waterworld, seaplane rides and, of course, the F1 circuit. Few people, however, ever get to see the gentler charms of this desert island. This walk seeks out the more relaxed pursuits on offer in this neighbourhood of shallow waters and mangrove forests.

❶ Breakfast at Nolu's

A good way to savour a lazy day is over breakfast at waterside **Nolu's** (☏02-557 9500; www.noluscafe.com; Al Bandar; meals Dh100; ☺8am-10pm Sat-Wed, to 11pm Thu & Fri). With its starburst abstract panels and its lime green decor, it feels more California than Abu Dhabi, but the secret recipes of the owner's Afghani mother gives a regional twist to the menu.

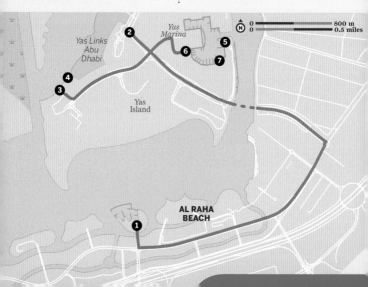

2 Pedalling on Yas

On the way from Al Bandar to Yas Island, note the Aldar HQ, the only circular building in the Middle East. Shaped like the wheel of a giant penny-farthing, it dominates the skyline. Talking of cycle wheels, if we're to live up to a gentle approach to the day, hire a bike from **Funride** (☑02-445 5838, 02-441 3264; www.funridesports.com; Crowne Plaza, Yas Island; per hr adult/child Dh30/20; ⏰9am-8pm, tour 6-9pm Tue & Wed) and enjoy the well-crafted cycle track (complete with water stations) running around the main sights of Yas Island or simply pedal to the next destination.

3 Exploring the Mangrove

Time to swap pedals for paddles and let the water soothe away your troubles. Specialising in local exploration, **Noukhada Adventure Company** (☑02- 558 1889; http://noukhada.ae; Yas Beach, Yas Island; kayaking tours adult/child from Dh220/170, minimum of 4; ⏰8.30am-5.30pm) runs popular kayaking trips through the local mangrove swamps. A 90-minute mangrove tour is a great way to experience this unusual habitat and get eye-to-eye with the herons who live there.

4 Grill & Chill at Yas Beach

Time for a bit of R&R after the upper-arm work, so moor up at **Yas Beach** (☑07-534 8729; www.yasbeach.ae; Yas Island; adult/child Dh100/free, half price Sun-Wed; ⏰10am-7pm Sun-Wed, to 10pm Fri & Sat), a delightfully low-key part of this high-tech island. The kitchen rustles up grilled local fish and other tasty light bites, chilled beer is available and a DJ plays soothing sounds on Friday. Day admission includes towel, sunbed, parasol and showers.

5 H2O Activities

Head over to Yas Circuit Marina and look up **Watercooled** (☑02- 406 2022; www.watercooleddubai.com/abu-dhabi; Yas Marina). Offering everything from wakeboarding to SUP (stand-up paddleboard) yoga, this company is reputedly the best for watersports in the UAE. Powerboating instruction is also offered.

6 Promenade Shopping

Walk off your sea legs with a stroll along the promenade. If you're around on a Saturday afternoon, enjoy a browse round Yas Marina's open-air **Saturday Market** (info@tinybeanevents.com; Yas Marina; ⏰1-6pm Sat), which features crafts, printed cottons, water-colour paintings, novelty gifts and souvenirs from stalls arranged along the promenade. The musical fountains will keep the kids' attention while you shop.

7 Cruising into the Sunset

Head for Gangway 3 of the Marina and book a cruise with **Captain Tony's** (☑02-650 7175; http://captaintonys.ae; Yas Marina; 90min sunset cruise adult/child Dh250/150; ⏰4.30pm, times vary with season), a company that takes an environmentally friendly approach to their tours. There's just enough time to join their popular sunset cruise.

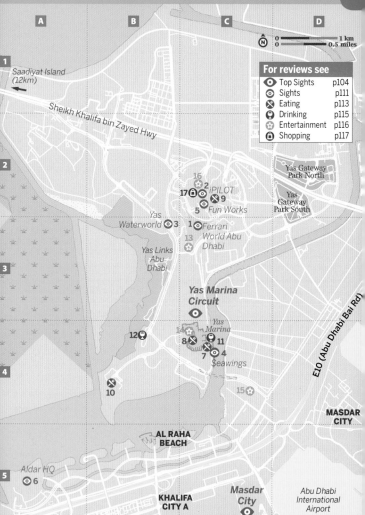

A B C D

For reviews see

◉	Top Sights	p104
◉	Sights	p111
✖	Eating	p113
🍷	Drinking	p115
★	Entertainment	p116
🛍	Shopping	p117

Saadiyat Island (12km)

Sheikh Khalifa bin Zayed Hwy

Yas Gateway Park North

Yas Gateway Park South

16
17 2 iPILOT
9
5 Fun Works

Yas Waterworld 3

1 Ferrari World Abu Dhabi
13

Yas Links Abu Dhabi

Yas Marina Circuit ◉

Yas Marina
14
12 8 11
7 4
Seawings
10

15

MASDAR CITY

E10 (Abu Dhabi Bai Rd)

AL RAHA BEACH

Aldar HQ
6

KHALIFA CITY A

Masdar City ◉

Abu Dhabi International Airport

0 ___ 1 km
0 ___ 0.5 miles

FATSEYEVA/SHUTTERSTOCK ©

Ferrari World Abu Dhabi, designed by Benoy

Sights

Ferrari World
Abu Dhabi
AMUSEMENT PARK

1 ⊙ Map p110, C3

If you want bragging rights to having 'done' Formula Rossa, the world's fastest roller coaster, visit this temple of torque and celebration of all things Ferrari in a spectacular building on Yas Island. Accelerating from zero to 240km/h in 4.9 seconds, this is as close to an F1 experience as most of us are likely to get.

Tamer diversions include a flume ride through a V12 engine, a motion-simulator that lets you ride shotgun with a racecar champion, and an imaginative 4D adventure. There's also a somewhat saner roller coaster that has you 'race' a Ferrari F430 Spider around the track. Between thrills, check out the car exhibitions or live shows.

(☏02-496 8000; www.ferrariworldabu dhabi.com; Yas Island; adult/child under 1.3m Dh250/205, premium admission Dh450/365; ◷11am-8pm, seasonal variations)

iPILOT
FLIGHT SIMULATOR

2 ⊙ Map p110, C2

Ever fancied landing an Airbus A380 or a Boeing 737 at Kai Tak Airport in Hong Kong (or 24,000 other airports around the world)? Now it's possible with the help of experienced pilots in the cockpit

Understand
Mangroves

The Eastern Mangroves off the northeast coast of Abu Dhabi are the largest mangrove forest in the UAE. Some key facts:

What is a mangrove? A mangrove is a subtropical, low-growing tree with high salt toleration that lives with roots immersed in the high tide.

Are all mangroves the same? No, there are 110 species. The grey mangrove is the most common in Abu Dhabi.

Why are they protected? This fragile ecosystem is a haven for wildlife and shelters coastlines from tidal erosion.

Who lives in these forests? Mangroves provide a safe breeding ground for shrimp, turtles and some fish species; they're also habitats for migrating birds.

Any other uses? Historically, they provided a rich source of fuel and building materials. The hard wood is resistant to rot and termites making it ideal for building boats and houses.

Are they endangered? Thanks to conservation efforts and deliberate re-planting schemes, mangrove stands have grown in size over recent years.

Are visits possible? Many tour companies organise trips into the Eastern Mangroves, particularly from Yas Island.

of these flight simulators – this is one heck of a ride. A fear-of-flying program is also available. Book online. (✆50-507 5660; www.flyipilot.ae; Yas Mall, Yas Island West; 15min Dh349)

Yas Waterworld   WATER PARK

3 ◉ Map p110, B3

The UAE's most elaborate water park offers opportunities to get soaked on 43 rides, slides and other liquid attractions as you follow Emirati cartoon character Dana on her quest for a magical pearl. A wave pool, two

lazy rivers and sunbeds offer relaxing alternatives to the rides if you're just looking to beat the Gulf heat.

With four thrill levels, there are rides for the fearful as well as the fearless. Top draws include the Bandit Bomber roller coaster with water and laser effects; a hair-raising slide called Liwa Loop; and Dawwama, a wild tornado ride through a 20m-high funnel that takes a gravity-defying 1½ minutes. Body sliding is also on offer. In contrast to other water parks, Yas Waterworld, with its attractive date-palm landscaping, leaves you in no doubt about your destination: there's even a pearl-diving show, *barasti* shelters and a souq to complement the heritage theme.

(☏02-414 2000; www.yaswaterworld.com; Yas Island; adult/child Dh240/195, fast pass Dh440/365; ☉10am-6pm Nov-Feb, to 7pm Mar-May, Sep & Oct, to 8pm Jun-Aug)

Seawings   SCENIC FLIGHTS

4 Map p110, C4

If you like to make a bit of a splash on entry, then consider arriving in Yas Island by seaplane. The scenic tour takes 25 minutes and takes off from the sea at either the Emirates Palace or Yas Marina. Book online.

(☏01-120 0000; www.seawings.ae; Yas Marina; scenic tour per person Dh895)

Fun Works   RIDES

5 Map p110, C2

With bouncy buildings, rides, rooms to reconstruct, play stations and toys, the 6300 sq metres of interactive play targeted at fun learning is guaranteed to keep kids amused for hours.

(☏02-565 1242; www.funworks.ae; Yas Mall, Yas Island West; ☉9am-10pm)

Aldar HQ   BUILDING

6 Map p110, A5

This remarkable building dubbed 'The Coin' has become a landmark of the Abu Dhabi suburbs, visible from afar and highly distinctive given its giant penny-shaped architecture.

The world's first circular skyscraper, this slender-width monument to modern design houses Aldar, one of the largest property developers in the Emirates.

(Al Bandar)

Eating

Aquarium   SEAFOOD $$

7 Map p110, C4

With stunning floor-to-ceiling aquariums gracing the interior of this casual-dining restaurant, there's no doubting its speciality. With indoor and outdoor seating, it makes a lovely lunchtime venue for Arabian-caught, Asian-prepared seafood, including sushi and sashimi on Sunday. Themed nights (including classic English fish and chips) are about to broaden the menu further.

(☏02-917 5605; Yas Marina; dishes Dh60; ☉noon-midnight)

☑ Top Tip

Eating & Drinking on Yas

There are dozens of restaurants, cafes and bars on Yas, so much so that the island almost deserves its own separate guidebook. An official website (www.yasisland.ae) gives a useful summary of all the options on offer, most of which are clustered around the marina, in Yas Mall and in each of the hotels.

Understand

Abu Dhabi's Black Gold

You only have to sniff the air during race weekend at Yas Marina Circuit to know that this is a city that loves its fuel!

Abu Dhabi's Oil Wealth

The oil reserves of the UAE are estimated at 98 billion barrels, 92 billion of which belong to Abu Dhabi. Within the space of 50 years, oil has transformed the capital from a fishing village into, according to the Sovereign Wealth Fund, the richest city in the world. With US$773 billion in cash and over US$10 trillion invested in overseas assets, it's little wonder that this wealthy Emirate is able to splash out. But where does all the oil come from?

Origins

Extensive flooding millions of years ago led to the remains of marine life being deposited in layers of sediment across Arabia's landmass. When dead organic matter is trapped under the land's surface with no oxygen, it is unable to decompose as it normally would. This forms the raw material of hydrocarbons – the origin of oil and gas.

   The conversion from dead organic matter to hydrocarbon is subject to many conditions, such as depth and temperature. Arabia's geology is uniquely supportive of these conditions, and nodding donkeys (oil pumps, capable of bringing oil to the surface from deep below ground) can be seen throughout the interior. In Abu Dhabi's dhow harbour, you can sometimes spot offshore platforms that have been towed in for maintenance.

How Long Will the Reserves Last?

Newspapers across the region agonise over reserves reaching their peak and whether modern technologies such as fracking will reduce the dependency on Arab oil. Given that the economies of the Gulf rely to a lesser or greater extent on oil and gas, this is one issue that can't be left to *insha'allah* (God's will). As such, Abu Dhabi and her neighbours are busy diversifying their economies and actively exploring alternative technologies (for example in Masdar City) to ensure they exchange today's black gold for tomorrow's well-founded future.

Cipriani ITALIAN $$$

8 Map p110, C4

The cuisine at this renowned restaurant may be Italian (including a lot of signature dishes from world-famous Harry's Bar in Venice) but the view is distinctly Emirates. The terrace looks out over the grandstands of the Yas Marina Circuit, designer yachts moored alongside and the Yas Viceroy hotel, with its mantel of amethyst and diamond lights.
(02-657 5400; www.cipriani; Yas Marina; mains around Dh150; 6pm-midnight)

Rogo's BURGERS $$

9 Map p110, C2

If you haven't got the stomach for Ferrari World, you may muster more of an appetite for this novel roller-coaster restaurant. Two conveyor belts deliver your meal from the kitchen via a pair of 12m-high tornado (spiral), double-loops, lifts and other engineering wizardry. Food of indifferent flavour is delivered in metal pots on plastic trays, and ordered via tablet.
(02-565 0888; www.rollercoasterrestaurant.com; Level 1, Yas Mall, Yas Island West; meals around Dh55; noon-11pm)

C.Deli SANDWICHES $

10 Map p110, B4

If you don't fancy a full dinner at a restaurant but would still like something tasty, then the all-day deli concept at the Rotana gives you the flexibility of

Aldar HQ (p113), designed by MZ Architects

a gourmet snack that you can take to your own favourite Yas Island haunt.
(02-656 4444; Centro Yas Island; sandwiches around Dh35; 24hr)

Drinking

Iris BAR

11 Map p110, C4

The wooden outdoor furniture gives a rustic feel to this relaxed bar in the heart of Yas Island. With occasional live jazz adding to the mellow atmosphere, this a companionable venue for sundowners.
(55-160 5636; www.irisabudhabi.com; Yas Marina; 6pm-3am)

Stills Bar & Brasserie BAR

 12 Map p110, B4

Boasting the longest bar in Abu Dhabi and with live entertainment, this is a lively spot for a cocktail. (02-656 3053; www.ichotelsgroup.com; Crowne Plaza, Yas Island; ⊙noon-1am, Ladies' Night 8-11pm Thu)

Entertainment

Du Arena CONCERT VENUE

 13 Map p110, C3

This exceptional outdoor entertainment venue (formerly known as Yas Arena) regularly hosts the big names of the regional and Western music world. With excellent acoustics and a unique cooling system, this venue has become one of the must-do stops on international tours. Tickets are available through the UAE Ticketmaster website. (02-509 8000; www.live.du.ae; www.ticketmaster.ae; Yas Island)

Burlesque Restaurant & Lounge CABARET

14 Map p110, C4

The star of the show at this red-velvet venue with scarlet, high-backed sofas and opulent drapes is the Friday cabaret (9.30pm to 11.30pm), with extravagant singing, dancing and live acts.

Understand
Water, Water Everywhere?

With palm-lined avenues, parks and flowerbeds, it's easy to forget that Abu Dhabi is built atop one of the most arid deserts on earth. The city receives no more than one or two days of rain per year, and the ground water is highly saline – almost eight times as much as sea water. All of the city's drinking water thus needs to come from desalination.

You'd think that the lack of natural reserves would have led to low water usage, but in fact the city has one of the highest per capita rates of water consumption in the world. Recognising the challenges involved in indulging the city's seemingly endless thirst for water, the government launches periodic awareness campaigns to encourage its citizens to consume less.

Visitors can play their part through the following simple measures:

▸ Showering rather than bathing.

▸ Cutting down on the laundry of towels and bed linens.

▸ Using, where possible, the half-flush button fitted as standard on most toilets.

▸ Turning off the tap when brushing your teeth.

From 11.30pm join centre stage with the after show party's glamorous DJs. (☏056-498 7580; www.burlesqueuae.com; Viceroy Yas Abu Dhabi, Yas Island; show/set menu per person Dh400; ⊗7pm-2am Sat & Mon-Wed, to 4am Thu & Fri)

O1NE
DANCE

 15 ⭐ Map p110, C4

For clubbers, this is one venue clearly remembered in the morning. A total of 19 international graffiti artists used 6000 cans to spray-paint the 3000-sq-metre exterior walls of the club. Arrive in style in a matching limousine and enjoy world-class artists and six resident DJs doing their thing in a unique interior of 3D projected images. (☏052-788 8111; www.o1neyasisland.com; Yas Island; ⊗11pm-late Thu & Fri)

Vox Cinemas
CINEMA

16 ⭐ Map p110, C2

If you like to smell the rubber on your car chase and feel the earth rumble as screaming tyres race across a 24.5m screen, then the 4D experience at Vox Cinema's XD Theatre won't disappoint. Book online. (☏600 599 905; uae.voxcinemas.com; Level 1, Yas Mall, Yas Island West; tickets from around Dh35; ⊗9am-midnight)

Shopping

Yas Mall
MALL

 17 🔒 Map p110, C2

Bright and spacious and with 55 trees and a growing plant wall, Yas Mall is the latest addition to the Abu Dhabi mega-shopping scene. Look out for two 12m-high tree-themed sculptures by acclaimed South African artist Marco Cianfanelli, with leaves inspired by Arabic calligraphy. There's access to Ferrari World, cinemas, Xtreme Zone entertainment and a Géant hypermarket. (☏toll free 800 927 6255; www.yasmall.ae; Yas West; ⊗10am-10pm Sat-Wed, to midnight Thu & Fri)

Top Sights
Abu Dhabi Falcon Hospital

Getting There

🚗 About 6km south-east of Abu Dhabi airport.

🚗 Follow Airport Rd (E20) in the direction of Falah City. About 3km past the junction with Hwy E11, turn right (before exit 30A).

Standing by the front door of the hospital watching anxious owners from across the region delivering their hooded 'patients' in person, it doesn't take long to realise that this is a much needed and much loved facility. Falcons are an integral part of traditional Gulf culture, and no expense is spared in restoring these magnificent birds to full health as a visit to this fascinating falcon hospital (the largest of its kind) shows.

Abu Dhabi Falcon Hospital

Don't Miss

Origins of Falconry

Falconry is an ancient art that dates from at least the 7th century BC. The first falconer, according to Arabic tradition, was a violent king of Persia who was so entranced by the grace and beauty of a falcon taking a bird on the wing that he had it captured so he could learn from it. What he learnt, according to legend, changed him into a calm and wise ruler.

Flight Training

It is no easy task to train birds of prey. Bedu, the falconers par excellence, traditionally net their falcons (usually saker or peregrine) during their migrations, using pigeons as bait. They train the birds through complex schedules of sleep deprivation and sparse feeding, retain them for as long as it takes to harvest fresh meat, and then set them free again at the onset of summer.

A Bond for Life

It is estimated that 2000 falcons are employed on the Arabian Peninsula each year. Today, birds are more usually bred and 'imprinted' from hatchlings to create a bond that lasts a lifetime. Sporting achievement is measured not through the number of quarry caught but in the skill of the catch – and in the wisdom of leaving enough prey for tomorrow.

Meeting, Beak to Beak

Guided tours include a visit to the falcon museum, the examination room and the free-flight aviary. You can watch a bird have a pedicure and, if you're willing to brave an arm, these well-behaved raptors will perch with you for the ultimate selfie.

☑ 02-575 5155

www.falconhospital.com

Al Raha

90min tour adult/child Dh170/60

⏲ tours 2pm Sat, 10am & 2pm Sun-Thu

☑ Top Tips

▶ Tour reservations (bookable online) are mandatory.

▶ Don't miss the Arabian Saluki Centre, which you can visit for free in the same complex.

▶ If you have 90-minutes to spare, nearby Masdar City (p106), a green community and research centre close to the airport, is well worth a visit. Tours are available online.

✗ Take a Break

The standard tour of the Falcon Hospital comes with refreshments.

The comprehensive tour comes with a buffet lunch in an Arab tent within the Falcon Hospital complex.

Top Sights
Arabian Saluki Centre

Getting There

🚗 About 6km southeast of Abu Dhabi airport.

🚗 Follow Airport Rd (E20) in the direction of Falah City. About 3km past the junction with Hwy E11, turn right (before exit 30A).

You'll probably hear the dogs before you see them as a howl goes up whenever a visitor approaches this hound pound. A visit here involves entering the kennels, meeting the affectionate and well looked-after residents, picking up a puppy or two and perhaps watching bath time. Prized by the Bedu for their hunting skills and their speed over long distances, salukis have for centuries been man's best friend. After a visit to this breeding and training centre, it's easy to see why.

Emirati men with their Arabian saluki dogs

Don't Miss

The Bedu's Best Friend

Originating in China, the saluki is thought to be one of the first breeds of dog to be domesticated. Their speed, tolerance of high temperatures and intelligence made them the perfect companions for nomadic communities who used them to catch rabbits and other small game. Some have been known to take down a small gazelle.

Fastest Four Legs

While there's not much call for their skills in the desert these days, they remain a beloved part of Bedouin heritage. Many are bred to race and, according to Guinness World Records, a saluki holds the record for sustained four-legged speed at 68.8 km/h, clocked in 1996. They can keep up high speeds over a distance of 6km.

Barking Beautiful

Salukis are not just admired for their speed, their beauty is also prized and dogs are paraded before the judges for their pride, stride and condition of coat. The major distinction is between 'feathered' (fine tufts of shaggy hair on their ears and tail) and 'smooth' (without tufts); many sport distinctive dark eyebrows.

Role of the Centre

Dedicated staff help train the dogs to catch (but not kill) rabbits and enhance their obedience – a bit of a lost cause given the dogs' independent spirit. With an active breeding program and boarding facilities for salukis belonging to city-dwelling owners, the centre helps keep the traditional relationship between master and hound alive.

☎ 02-575 5330

www.arabiansaluki.ae

admission free

☑ Top Tips

▶ Wear old clothing if you want to get up close and personal with these affectionate dogs.

▶ To see these wonderful, sleek dogs in action, visit the 10-day Al Dhafra Festival, in Madinat Zayed in the emirate's western region.

✕ Take a Break

The centre offers coffee and dates to visitors, but there are no other facilities for eating at the complex. If you book a comprehensive package at the neighbouring Falcon Hospital (p118), a buffet lunch is included.

The ecofriendly Masdar City (p106) is close by and offers a range of healthy treats at Organic Foods and Café (p107).

The Best of
Abu Dhabi

Interior of Sheikh Zayed Grand Mosque (p90)
BEATRICE PREVE/ALAMY ©

Best Walks
Walking the Abu Dhabi Corniche

🏃 The Walk

Stroll along the sea, enjoying the landscaped gardens of the Corniche, singing birds and scented trees, and soon the busy metropolis will seem a world away. That said, there isn't a better way to admire the modern architecture of downtown Abu Dhabi. Attempt this route in the early morning or evening in summer to avoid the excessive heat.

Start Abu Dhabi Flag; 🚌 Marina Mall bus stop

Finish Heritage Park; 🚌 Sheraton bus stop

Length 10.5km; four hours

🍴 Take a Break

There are refreshment kiosks around the public beaches of the western Corniche, but carry water for the eastern half. Pause mid-route at the friendly Nova Beach Café (p54), but beware, once settled in you may not want to move!

Abu Dhabi Corniche (p24)

LATITUDESTOCK/FRANK FELL/GETTY IMAGES IMAGES ©

❶ Abu Dhabi Heritage Village

From the giant flag, the symbol of unity in this capital city, it's a brief stroll to the **Abu Dhabi Heritage Village** (p42). Here you can enjoy a glimpse of Emirati life before oil revenues transformed the country forever.

❷ Breakwater

Stroll along the breakwater. The view beyond is dominated by the opulent **Emirates Palace** (p40) – hotel, spa, cultural centre and general city icon.

❸ Etihad Towers

Joining the Corniche, you'll notice a billboard-sized poster of Sheikh Zayed, father of the nation. His 'benign dictatorship' brought great development to Abu Dhabi and the country as a whole, as demonstrated by the architectural optimism of buildings like the **Etihad Towers** (p146) clustered opposite.

❹ Corniche Beach

Walking along the Corniche (or you can cycle from here), you'll see similar expressions of confidence, such as Nation Towers, home to the St Regis. The Hiltonia and the Nation Riviera Beach Clubs offer luxurious swimming; the **Corniche Beach** (p30) is free and blue-flagged for its cleanliness.

5 World Trade Centre

Take a break at the Nova Beach Café and pause next at Rashid Bin Saeed Al Maktoum St. The inland procession of fine buildings includes the **Burj Mohammed bin Rashid**

(p30), the city's tallest tower and home to the World Trade Centre, and the Etisalat building with its 'golf ball' crown.

6 Al Markaziah Gardens (East)

This stretch is beautifully landscaped and parallels attractive gardens, like **Lake Park** (p27), inland. Underpasses connect the two sides of the road.

7 Sheraton Lagoon

In a city where the shoreline has been

dredged and reshaped at will, it's endearing to see that the *khor* (desert lagoon) beside the **Sheraton** (p68) has not been filled in. In fact, the Corniche passes over it leaving this venerable hotel with its treasured beach.

8 Dhow Harbour

You could end here (there's a cycle station and a bus stop by the Sheraton) or continue on to **Heritage Park** (p68) and a romantic view of the dhows floating two-abreast in the harbour opposite.

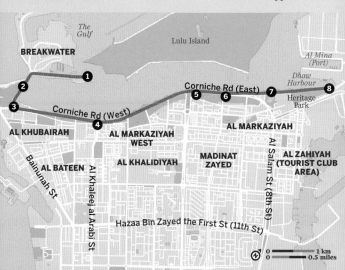

Best Walks
Markets & Malls

🏃 The Walk

Like many Gulf cities, Abu Dhabi has a penchant for malls. And for good reason. Collected under a roof, shaded against the heat and offering a single stop for most of life's necessities (eating, drinking, shopping and socialising), they provide a solution to life *in extremis*. This walk traces the origins of the mall in the city's early markets and ends in one of the capital's favourites.

Start Al Mina; 🚌 Al Mina bus stop

Finish Abu Dhabi Mall; 🚌 Abu Dhabi bus stop

Length 5.8km; 2½ hours

🍴 Take a Break

The obvious place for a break at lunchtime is Al Arish Restaurant (p85), near the fish market, which offers an extensive and authentic Emirati buffet.

MATILDE GATTONI/GETTY IMAGES ©

Abu Dhabi Mall (p72)

❶ Dates Alley

Everybody in the region will tell you the best dates are from their home town and then list the features of their favourite variety. Learn more about this life-supporting food at the **Fruit and Vegetable Market** (p79).

❷ Hardware Stores

Dates play an important part of the famous Arab coffee ritual and are served at social functions. A coffee pot and thumbnail cups make the perfect souvenir and can be bought from among the pots and pans of the **Iranian Souq** (p79).

❸ Fish Souq

You'll notice cacti for sale in the neighbouring nurseries, but contrary to expectations they don't grow in Gulf deserts. This is because in summer there's little difference between day and night temperatures. The water, too, remains uniformly warm, leading to an abundance of marine life – much of which is on sale at the **Fish Market** (p79).

4 Dhow Harbour

You'll have noticed lots of crustaceans being sold in the Fish Market. The Arabian Gulf is famous for lobsters and crayfish, which until recently were discarded by Emirati in favour of tuna and sardines. You can see from the number of lobster pots by the **dhow harbour** (p81) that their value is now recognised!

5 Carpet Souq

Dhows are handcrafted and adapted to the character of their skipper, but they invariably have one thing in common – an old rug thrown over the timbers and a handful of cushions. See where these workaday textiles are bought in the nearby **Carpet Souq** (p78).

6 Khalifa Centre

For a much more refined version of carpets and *kilims,* stride out to the **Khalifa Centre** (p73; 30-minute walk). This 20th-century collection of independent shops bridges the gap between old market and modern mall and encompasses Oriental carpets and

crafts from across the region.

7 Abu Dhabi Mall

Wondering what's for sale from the Emirates in the Khalifa Centre? You're looking in the wrong place! The Gulf ports have for centuries been used as conduits for silks from India and spices from Africa. Hence the multinational flavour of the city's modern shopping emporiums, like the **Abu Dhabi Mall** (p72) opposite.

Best
Eating

Built on islands, it is inevitable that seafood features highly in the cuisine of Abu Dhabi. But there is more to local flavours than king fish or fillet of *hammour*. Sampling the cuisine of the regional expatriate communities who have helped build the capital is a highlight, with Indian and Lebanese food scoring high on the list for good value.

LARA FERRONI/GETTY IMAGES ©

Where to Eat

Abu Dhabi's top fine-dining restaurants tend to be found in the five-star hotels and newer shopping malls. In contrast, the streets one block south of Zayed the First St, between Al Markaziah West and Al Manhal, present a geography of regional cuisine from Syria to Yemen, with each independent eatery occupying its own shopfront.

What to Eat

Abu Dhabi is a great city for sampling traditional Middle Eastern food. This usually involves small hot and cold dishes (mezze), such as hummus, *muttabal* (purée of aubergine) and *sambusak* (cheese-filled pastries), which are enjoyed over long chats and a watermelon juice to aid digestion. This is followed by rice and meat in various preparations with unleavened bread. Dessert is an afterthought.

When to Eat

A much loved city tradition is Friday brunch. This lavish buffet starts mid-morning and continues to mid-afternoon. Afternoon tea is another Abu Dhabi favourite offering an affordable opportunity to enjoy a fine-dining environment. Dinner cruises set sail in the early evening, but most locals pile into the coffeehouses for light bites, coffee and *sheesha* late into the night.

Best Seafood

Scott's This award-winning restaurant with its romantic outdoor terrace offers extravagant sea views. (p51)

Vasco's The Vasco twist at this relaxed lunch venue is a reminder of the region's Portuguese influence. (p45)

Turquoiz A romantic sundowner of a restaurant on Saadiyat Beach. (p86)

Sayad Possibly the city's finest seafood in the city's most celebrated hotel. (p53)

Best Local Ambience

Café Arabia The villa's modern but the Arab welcome is of ancient lineage. (p98)

Living Room Café Craving for something baked from mum's kitchen? The family will love it here. (p52)

Zyara Cafe Come for mezze in this riot of colour overlooking the Corniche. (p27)

Cho Gao A friendly city crowd piles into this pan-Asian restaurant for after-work socials. (p27)

Al Mina Modern Cuisine & Restaurant A little-known gem beside the dhow harbour. (p79)

Best Value

Al Ibrahimi Restaurant Watch expatriate local life pass by the tables of this popular Indian street restaurant. (p33)

Automatic Restaurant An institution in the Gulf, whole heads of lettuce come free with Lebanese grills. (p69)

Lebanese Flower One of dozens of regional shwarma, grill and pastry shops near Qasr Al Hosn. (p32)

Best Regional Flavours

Al Arish Restaurant A lunchtime of Emirati favourites is served daily at this flamboyantly Arabian restaurant. (p126)

Al Asala Heritage Restaurant Popular with tour groups, this Heritage Village restaurant offers Emirati dishes. (p52)

Mezlai Mashed spuds with camel's milk? Only the Emirates Palace could get away with it. (p53)

Mijana Offering six varieties of hummus and raw minced lamb, Mijana appeals to a sophisticated palette. (p98)

Best Local Traditions

Giornotte Forget anything but a snooze after the best brunch in town. (p101)

Ushna Join those in the know for a curry lunch with a grand mosque view. (p99)

Best Novel Experiences

Beach House Overlooking a coastal reserve, crabs may join the party. (p86)

18° Contemplate the angle of dangle over supper in the leaning tower. (p98)

Aquarium Wall-to-ceiling fish tanks are a talking point in this Yas favourite. (p113)

Rogo's Acrobatic lunch plates are delivered to the table by conveyor belt. (p115)

Worth a Trip

It might seem daft to recommend **Suhail** (02-886 2088; www.qasralsarab. anantara.com; Qasr Al Sarab, near Hameem, off E90 (Liwa Rd); mains Dh220; 7-10.30pm), a restaurant 200km from the city, but arriving at the fairy-tale Qasr Al Sarab is a great adventure that makes the two-hour drive through the sand dunes worthwhile. Serving the very best cuts of beef from around the world and an award-winning wine list, Suhail offers a night to remember.

Best
Nightlife

In a country of extreme temperatures, it's hardly surprising that the pace of life by day is slow. City dwellers make up for it at night, however, pouring onto the Corniche for a constitutional at dusk and sitting out until late sipping coffee and smoking *sheesha*. Visitors are welcome to join this regime or gravitate towards Western bars popular with expats.

GROWTOGRAPH BY JOY BUTLER/GETTY IMAGES ©

Local Style

If you think of the picnic as an essentially daytime activity, then think again. The Emiratis, in common with people of the Gulf in general, love big parties. These generally involve going out en mass with the extended family, finding a comfortable perch, preferably outdoors, and chatting until the small hours. These ad hoc nighttime picnics in Abu Dhabi's parks form the focus of city nightlife for many locals.

The Expat Way

Abu Dhabi abounds with favourite expat watering holes and most midrange and top-end restaurants and hotels have bars serving alcohol. Nightlife for Western expats tends to revolve around these haunts, many of which offer promotions, sports on TV, ladies' nights, cocktail menus and rooftop lounges. Resident DJs put in an appearance later at night and bands, generally from the Philippines, add a bit of boogie to the beat.

Doing Your Own Thing

To enjoy the best of both worlds, follow local custom and pitch up at the park with a barbecue supper. Chase it down with coffee and a *sheesha* at a local Corniche cafe and then call into a bar for a nightcap.

☑ Top Tips

▶ Alcohol can only be consumed in licensed restaurants and bars or in a private home.

▶ The consumption of alcohol is restricted during Ramadan and on religious holidays.

▶ Although haram in Islam, alcohol consumption is left to individual conscience.

▶ Mocktails are an art form in capital bars.

Best Sundowners

De La Costa Relax in an armchair and you can almost hear the turtles coming ashore. (p86)

Iris An island of low-tech on an island of high-tech, this venue has great sunset views. (p115)

Ray's Bar At the top of the glamorous Jumeirah, this bar could be renamed Sun Rays – it's a good spot to catch the last of them. (p58)

Best Sheesha Cafes

Café Layali Zaman A regional crowd pleaser, it's lively until the small hours. (p35)

Colombiano Coffee House When the seaside is too humid, this inland haunt catches a breeze. (p27)

Tiara Resto Café Perennially busy, this is a classic coffee and a *sheesha* hangout. (p36)

Best Nightlight Views

Bentley Bistro & Bar Abu Dhabi looks dazzling at night from this upper-crust bar on Al Maryah Island. (p69)

Arabic Café An early nighter of a cafe, the evening views of Breakwater are fun. (p57)

Al Bateen Resort Yacht Club With uninterrupted views of the capital skyline, this is a *sheesha* classic. (p55)

Havana Café & Restaurant Rough and ready, the fine views are an unexpected bonus of this coffeehouse. (p45)

Best Lounge Life

Etoiles The city often tells a story of rags to riches, but you'll only see the latter here! (p55)

Stills Bar & Brasserie With the longest bar in the city, you'll never be short of a perch. (p116)

Stratos You haven't had one too many – the lounge really does revolve. (p27)

Best Expat Haunts

Ally Pally Corner A man cave from the oil-pioneering days when it was almost the only pub in town. (p69)

Belgian Beer Café Can't be beaten for hops, mussels and home-cut chips. (p57)

Cooper's Ladies' night is virtually every night in this popular haunt. (p99)

Planet Café If beer and football is not your thing, then ludo and back-gammon here might do the trick. (p71)

Hemingway's An old-time favourite with a live band makes this a city institution. (p57)

Best Dancing

Eight International DJs get the floor popping in this upmarket club. (p100)

Relax@12 A drink here helps lubricate the legs for the dance floor next door. (p100)

Sax Don't attempt the venue's name after a drink or two. (p36)

Best High Tea

Observation Deck at 300 Offers high tea in an elevated venue on the 74th floor. (p55)

Le Café Afternoon tea here is a beloved local tradition where all that sparkles really is gold! (p54)

Best
Entertainment

From piano bars and Filipino bands to opera and international pop concerts, Abu Dhabi has plenty of 'what's on' to show off on your 'WhatsApp'. Most entertainment takes place in hotels and malls, but there are a couple of purpose-built venues of international standard on Yas Island where big-ticket celebs draw the crowds.

ALLAN BAXTER/GETTY IMAGES ©

Best Hotel Music

Giornotte Piano music accompanies the city's favourite brunch at the Ritz-Carlton. (p101)

Chameleon A resident DJ vies with the mixologist to provide the best entertainment at the Fairmont. (p101)

Cristal The old-world charm is matched by old world piano at the Millennium Hotel. (p36)

Best Stage Craft

Abu Dhabi Classics Ballet, opera and classical concerts with renowned orchestras are staged in the Emirates Palace auditorium. (p58)

Burlesque Slip into something black or red and enjoy the Friday cabaret. (p116)

Du Arena A key destination for many international artists on their world tours. (p116)

Best Bands & DJs

49er's The Gold Rush A resident DJ takes over where the local band leaves off. (p71)

Jazz Bar & Dining Live jazz bands entertain a sage audience at this old favourite. (p58)

People by Crystal Abu Dhabi Offers a chic night out with top theatrical and musical talents of the urban and house scene. (p86)

Best 3D & 4D Experiences

O1NE This contemporary dance space with its graffiti shell and 3D projections attracts top-name DJs. (p117)

☑ **Top Tips**

▶ Impress the friends by turning up at O1NE in a matching graffiti-painted limo.

▶ Tickets for concerts are available through the UAE's Ticketmaster website: www.ticketmaster.ae.

Vox Cinemas At the Marina and at Yas Malls, regular screenings of 3D and 4D films make for a sensory experience. (p58)

Grand Cinemas A popular Abu Dhabi Mall cinema showing Hollywood films. (p72)

Best
Shopping

Best Malls

Abu Dhabi Mall An ageing favourite, this mall has plenty of local interest with perfume, nut and Arab sweet shops. (p72)

Marina Mall Visit the Sky Tower, in the heart of the mall, for a good view out to sea. (p61)

Yas Mall Adjacent to Ferrari World, there are many restaurants here for a pit stop. (p117)

Best for Luxury Goods

Avenue at Etihad Big fashion houses ensure boutique shopping at its best. (p60)

Nation Galleria Worth visiting just for the tower it's housed in, this mall has many unique stores. (p59)

Paris Avenue See what's trending abroad in a boutique dedicated to up-and-coming designers. (p59)

The Galleria Part of the 'wow' factor in the Sow-wah Square complex on Al Maryah Island. (p73)

Best for Regional Souvenirs

Souq Central Market Built on the site of the original souq, this Norman Foster arcade is a delight to visit. (p37)

Souq Qaryat al Beri With quality souvenirs, this modern take on the classic souq has a great waterfront location. (p101)

Khalifa Centre A ragbag of shops selling carpets, boxes, pashminas and brass coffee pots. (p73)

Best Local Interest

Carpet Souq Haggle hard for a hand-loomed *kilim* from the Baluchi traders. (p78)

Iranian Souq Selling pots and pans, plants and pillows, it's the teeming space that makes this souq fascinating. (p79)

Madinat Zayed Gold Centre All the gold shops of Abu Dhabi collected under one roof. (p36)

FRANK FELL/GETTY IMAGES ©

☑ **Top Tips**

▶ Traditionally Arab men buy women gold but wear silver.

▶ Mall etiquette dictates that knees and shoulders should be covered (men and women).

▶ Shows of affection are best avoided in malls and markets.

▶ Haggling means finding the price at which you're happy to buy and the vendor is happy to sell.

Best
Activities

Until recently, Abu Dhabi was known as the sedate Emirate with little to do but eat and watch the sun go down. Not anymore! With Yas Island bringing the F1 Grand Prix to town, the city has revved into action and there's now plenty to keep visitors of all ages and inclinations on the go.

STUART FORSTER/ALAMY ©

Full Throttle

Yas Island is the place to head to for thrill-seekers. The island offers opportunities to drive race cars on the Formula One circuit, to simulate flying, to experience g-force on the world's fastest roller coaster, and to get dunked, flung and whirlpooled into water from alarming heights. Booking online eliminates long waits.

Gentler Pursuits

Getting active in Abu Dhabi isn't just about being thrilled (or terrorised) by technology: it also involves gentler pursuits. Jogging in city parks, cycling along the Corniche, or teeing off on some beautiful, celebrity-designed golf courses are some of the many slower-paced, easily accessed activities available.

Waterborne Activities

The Arabian Gulf is the arena in which rush and hush combine. Famous for its annual F1 power-boat competition, the capital is a good place to learn to drive these spirited steeds of the water. A whole range of other watersports are on offer, from paddle power to pedalo, and the resorts offer kayaking, fishing trips and sunset cruises.

Best Adrenalin Rush

Yas Central A chance to skid your way round the famous Yas Marina Circuit. (p104)

Ferrari World Abu Dhabi Offering the fastest ride in the world, a go-kart academy and technically dazzling simulations. (p111)

Yas Waterworld Go in search of the lost pearl on over 40 slides and rides with an Arabian context. (pictured above; p112)

Best Dhow Cruise

Abu Dhabi Dhow Cruise A relaxing potter around the Breakwater in a traditional fishing vessel. (p81)

Abu Dhabi Pearl Journey Own a pearl at the end of this informative dhow journey. (p96)

Al Dhafra Dinner Cruise Popular sunset trips are also possible from the Dhow Harbour. (p85)

Best Airborne Activity

Abu Dhabi Helicopter Tour Go eye-to-eye with suspended window-cleaners during vertical take-off. (p51)

Seawings Land like ducks on the flat calm sea. (p113)

iPILOT Enjoy the thrill of piloting a big plane without the responsibility. (p111)

Best for Boats

Lulu Boats Charter a boat to an island paradise. (p45)

Shuja Yacht Dinner on board this beautiful vessel is a cut above the rest. (p45)

Belevari Catamarans Expect a party atmosphere on this feel-good craft. (p48)

Best for Watersports

Noukhada Adventure Company Stand-up paddling or sit down kayaking, this is the eco-way to enjoy the mangroves. (p109)

Watercooled If there's a new board, craft or kite out there, Watercooled has it covered, power-boats included. (p109)

Captain Tony's Famous for sunset cruises, Captain Tony offers bucket-and-spade tours for the ultimate R&R. (p109)

Best for Landlubbers

Funride Bikes are easy to hire from four stations on the Corniche and on Yas Island; the dedicated tracks make it safe for all. (p50)

Byky Bike Not too hot on two wheels? Share the effort with a friend in a variety of karts and buggies. (p97)

Zayed Sports City Hit an ace on the same court as your tennis idol or go bowling with the best. (p97)

Worth a Trip

A popular activity in the Emirate of Abu Dhabi is off-road driving in the desert, and most tour companies organise these exciting trips. If you're heading out for a 4WD excursion and fancy seeing other desert-adapted cars en route, call into **Emirates National Auto Museum** (☎ 05-749 2155; www.enam.ae; Hwy E65; Dh50; ⊙8am-6pm), a hangar-sized homage to the auto.

Best
Arts & Crafts

With Abu Dhabi's Cultural District taking shape on Saadiyat Island and the Louvre rumoured to open at the end of 2015, there's a surge of interest in contemporary arts in the capital. This is something of a novelty in a region more readily associated with a heritage of craft.

HEEB CHRISTIAN/AGEFOTOSTOCK ©

Best for Fine Arts

Barakat Gallery High-end art worth a browse. (p48)

Miraj Islamic Centre Museum-quality pieces open for view in this private collection. (p93)

Manarat Al Saadiyat A large exhibition space hosts international shows. (p76)

Best Contemporary Arts

Abu Dhabi Pottery Establishment A showcase for the collectable ceramics of Homa Vafaie-Farley. (p60)

Folklore Gallery Displays works by young local talent. (p59)

Ghaf Gallery A modern exhibition space set up by Emirati artist Jalal Luqman in partnership with Bahraini Mohammed Kanoo. (p60)

Best Browsing for Crafts

Eclectic An Aladdin's cave of antiques, furniture and textiles. (p59)

Saturday Market On Yas Island, this weekly market showcases local crafts. (p109)

Abu Dhabi Heritage Village Traditional crafts produced in village workshops. (p42)

Women's Handicraft Centre Government-run centre supporting local cottage industries. (p86)

☑ **Top Tips**

▶ If you're interested in the visual arts, plan your trip for November during the Abu Dhabi Contemporary Art Fair, hosted on Saadiyat Island.

▶ To find out what's on culturally, check the following website: www.culturein abudhabi.ae.

▶ In February, the Qasr Al Hosn Festival showcases Emirati heritage and culture with poetry reading, *oud* recitals and craft markets.

Best
Beaches & Spas

PAUL TODD/GETTY IMAGES ©

Surrounded by water on all sides, Abu Dhabi has made the most of its beachfront location. There are views out to sea from the resorts on Saadiyat Island and inland waters offer refreshing breezes. Beat the heat in summer with a spa, but bring a platinum credit card.

Best Public Beaches

Corniche Beach Gives opportunities for women and families to enjoy some privacy. Lifeguard available. (p30)

Saadiyat Public Beach A boardwalk leads through the protected nature sanctuary to a pristine beach. (p84)

Yas Beach A fun vibe and a great place to chill with a beer. (p109)

Best Beach Clubs

Hiltonia Health Club & Spa With shady palm trees, this is one of the city's most popular leisure facilities. (p49)

Nation Riviera Beach Club In a stylish cluster of buildings on the Corniche, offering a luxury day out. (p44)

Saadiyat Beach Club The infinity pool of this upmarket club is reason enough to visit. (p84)

Rotana Hotel & Towers Beach Club A low-key, pleasant beach to pause at between shopping trips. (p68)

Best Spas

Anantara Spa Housed in a celebration of marble, this spa includes a traditional Turkish hammam. (p96)

Sense A super-sophisticated, high-tech approach to indulgent bathing. (p67)

Emirates Palace Spa The ultimate in decadence, with 24kt gold applications. (p49)

☑ Top Tips

▶ Free public access to clean beaches is available along the Western Corniche.

▶ Day rates are offered at all the private beach clubs listed here.

▶ From May to September, the beach is too hot to sit on for most of the day.

▶ A hat, water and sunblock are essential year round.

Best
Architecture

Abu Dhabi's modern skyline is one of the most spectacular in the Middle East with exciting towers, aerial bridges and unusual exterior textures, representing not just outstanding design but also remarkable feats of engineering. In the capital, hotels and malls are not designed merely for function, they participate in the avant-garde aesthetic of the city.

Building on Sand

Survey the old photographs in the museum at the Abu Dhabi Heritage Village and you'll notice that less than a century ago Qasr Al Hosn was located in splendid isolation in the middle of an empty coastal plain. Today, this modest structure that once received emirs, ambassadors and royalty is dwarfed by the high-rises downtown. This gives a measure of the pace of development.

Humble Beginnings

The famous desert explorer Wilfred Thesiger writes of reaching a small town of 2000 inhabitants in the late 1940s after crossing the Empty Quarter. He led his faltering camels across the mud of the Al Maqtar Khor to reach the mainland as there were no bridges. Today, three bridges connect the mainland to Abu Dhabi Island and the city has grown to a population of around 2.5 million.

Future Vision

There are lots of ways of engaging with the city's architecture. Stroll or cycle along the city's two Corniches, around Yas Island and along Al Maryah Island Promenade, or take the Big Bus Tour. For a view of the future, a trip to Manarat Al Saadiyat is a must.

CHRISTIAN HACKER/GETTY IMAGES ©

☑ Top Tips

▶ Don't miss the street sculpture, giant symbols of the city's heritage, outside the World Trade Centre.

▶ Note that mosques don't follow the grid system – they're oriented to face Mecca.

Best Cultural Icons

Sheikh Zayed Grand Mosque This is the jewel in the crown of the capital. (p90)

Manarat Al Saadiyat Visit the permanent exhibition for an overview of the city's architectural vision. (p76)

Abu Dhabi Louvre The Louvre's interior features a rain of light. (p83)

Etihad Towers (p146)

UAE Pavilion This celebrated exhibition space is in the shape of two sand dunes. (p83)

Best Contemporary Structures

Aldar HQ Appearing like a giant penny on the approach to Yas Island, this is the only circular building in the Gulf. (p113)

Sowwah Square The focal point of the spectacular Al Maryah CBD developments. (p64)

Emirates Palace Bridging the gap between modern and traditional Arab architecture. (p40)

Viceroy Yas Abu Dhabi This hotel, with a mantel that dazzles at night, straddles the Yas Marina Circuit. (p104)

Masdar City Using recycled materials and focusing on energy efficiency, Masdar showcases ecofriendly architecture. (p106)

Sheikh Zayed Bridge Evocative of sand dunes, this intricate bridge almost seems to move at night. (p95)

Best City Towers

Jumeirah at Etihad Towers This beautiful cluster of towers punctuates the western end of the Corniche. (p146)

Burj Mohammed bin Rashid This is the highest building in Abu Dhabi, with a striking slanting roof. (p30)

Etisalat Headquarters A city landmark, the gold ball crown makes this building hard to miss. (p31)

Capital Gate Currently holds the world's record for the most extreme lean. (p96)

Best Heritage Architecture

Sheikh Zayed Centre One of the few examples of traditional Gulf architecture in the city. (p48)

Abu Dhabi Heritage Village Note the windtower, an inspiration for today's eco-aware architects. (p42)

Qasr Al Hosn This fort is the oldest, and was once the only, building in the city. (p30)

Al Maqta Fort & Watchtower Marooned in the modernity of Bain Al Jessrain. (p95)

Best
For Kids

With its many kids' zones in shopping malls and shaded parks, most with slides, swings and climbing frames, Abu Dhabi has lots of fun for the family. In addition, top class theme parks on Yas Island ensure that all ages are catered for. Don't forget some of the out-of-town features, such as the Arabian Saluki Centre, which introduce children to local culture.

VLADIMIR MELNIK/SHUTTERSTOCK ©

Best Mall Entertainment

Fun City Offering games and rides for pre-teens. (p51)

Fun Works Learning is the focus of this play environment. (p113)

Snow City Build an igloo in Yas Mall! (p117)

Best City Parks for Kids

Al Khalidiyah Public Park There are good climbing frames here. (p51)

Murjan Splash Park Safe interaction with water guns and slides in Khalifa Park. (p96)

Best Out-of-Town Experiences

Falcon Hospital A chance to learn about falcons and meet them up close. (p119)

Saluki Centre Cuddling the puppies is way too good for kids! (p121)

Best Transport

Byky Bike Get the kids mobile in a variety of carts. (p97)

Funride Offers bicycles and helmets for children. (p50)

Best for Eating

Living Room Café With a VIP children's menu, this is home away from home. (p52)

☑ **Top Tips**

▶ A warm layer is useful year round to avoid overly cold AC in malls and cold nights in winter.

▶ The heat of summer is hard for infants as dehydration is a danger. Hats are essential.

▶ Discounts are available for children. The cut-off age is usually 10 years old or dictated by height.

Rogo's Give the kids control of the ordering via iPad and watch the dishes arrive by roller coaster. (p115)

Best
Tours

There are all kinds of insightful tours of Abu Dhabi and its marine and desert environment to choose from. Most city and sea tours are between two hours and half a day. To make the most of desert trips, consider staying overnight.

Desert Safaris

These exciting tours offer an opportunity to learn about Bedouin traditions in the surrounding desert dunes. Try to avoid companies that promote 'dune bashing': 4WD trips are a legitimate way of exploring the desert but tearing up the dunes with speed is not the healthiest engagement with this fragile environment. Try the following operators:

Emirates Tours & Safari (www.eatours.ae)

Abu Dhabi Adventure (www.abudhabiadventure.com)

Arabian Adventures (www.arabian-adventures.com).

PETER RYAN / ROBERT HARDING ©

☑ Top Tips

▶ Binoculars are handy for spotting the rich migratory bird life.

▶ Dolphins are easily spotted early in the morning.

▶ Don't forget a warm layer for cool desert nights in winter.

Best City Tours

Big Bus Tour Stopping at all the city highlights, this hop-on, hop-off service comes with an audioguide. (p50)

Seawings Offering an aerial tour of the city, this plane takes off and lands on water. (p113)

Abu Dhabi Helicopter Tour Hover over the city's landmarks on 20- or 30-minute flights. (p51)

Best Boat Tours

Captain Tony's Runs environmentally informative ecotours to the mangroves. (p109)

Noukhada Adventure Company Runs full moon and ecotours through the mangroves by kayak. (p109)

Abu Dhabi Pearl Journey Learn about the city's pearling heritage on this dhow tour and keep an oyster at the end. (p96)

Abu Dhabi Dhow Cruise Tour the breakwater in a traditional dhow. (p81)

Best
Sporting Events

Abu Dhabi has become closely associated with the Formula One Grand Prix and as expected it brings true razzmatazz to the city. But this is not the only sporting event pulling in the crowds these days: tennis, Formula One power boating, ocean racing and camel racing are highlights of an ever-expanding sporting calendar.

MOHANNAD KHATIB @MEDIUMSHOT/GETTY IMAGES ©

Abu Dhabi Grand Prix

(📞02-659 9800; www.yasmarinacircuit.ae; ⏱Nov) This day-night race, the last in the F1 calendar, attracts visitors from around the globe.

Desert Master Trek

(www.liwachallenge.com; ⏱Feb) Spread over the high dunes of the Empty Quarter near Liwa, this gruelling sand race covers two distances, one 100km and one 200km, with a finale on the ridge of the highest dune.

Mubadala World Tennis Championship (www.mubadalawtc.com; Sheikh Zayed Sports City; ⏱Jan) With the best international players, including Djokovic, Nadal, Wawrinka and Murray,

participating, this is a key event at the start of the tennis year.

President's Cup Falcon Competition (www.fcad.ae; ⏱Jan) Displaying the skills of these impressive raptors, this competition highlights the intimate relationship with their owners. Prize money of Dh25 million and 56 cars are inducements to preserve this ancient sport.

Al Wathba Camel Races

(📞02-583 9200; Al Wathba; admission free; ⏱7.30am & 2.30pm Thu-Sat Oct-Apr) Sporting colourful nose bags and matching blankets, the camels are the stars of the show, encouraged along by their owners driving alongside.

☑ **Top Tips**

▶ Check dates on www.abudhabievents.ae, the official events calendar.

▶ Book tickets for the Abu Dhabi Grand Prix several months in advance.

XCAT World Series Powerboat Race (www.xcatracing.com; The Corniche; ⏱Dec) These 6000cc powerboats reach speeds of 120mph along the breakwater in front of the Abu Dhabi Corniche, making for an exhilarating spectacle.

Survival Guide

Survival Guide

Before You Go

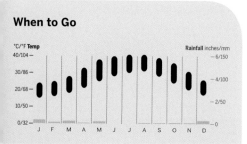

When to Go

°C/°F Temp
40/104 —
30/86 —
20/68 —
10/50 —
0/32 —
J F M A M J J A S O N D

Rainfall inches/mm
— 6/150
— 4/100
— 2/50
— 0

➡ **Winter (Dec–Feb)** A good season to visit but with chilly temperatures and the odd shower.

➡ **Spring (Mar–Apr)** One of the best times to visit with temperatures around 30°C.

➡ **Summer (May–Sep)** Avoid: temperatures average around 45°C with a stifling 95% humidity.

➡ **Autumn (Oct–Nov)** Temperatures fall leaving enough heat to remember you're in the desert but not enough to make visiting intolerable.

Book Your Stay

☑ **Top Tip** Don't skimp on accommodation if you don't have to. Instead of an average room, a few extra dirhams can deliver a once-in-a-lifetime experience.

➡ There are essentially two types of hotel in Abu Dhabi: beach resorts and city hotels.

➡ Beach hotels are generally five-star with private beaches and luxurious facilities.

➡ Midrange options cater to the business market with meeting facilities, internet access, wi-fi and gyms.

➡ Budget hotels are rare in Abu Dhabi, but respected budget chains such as Ibis offer clean rooms and efficient service.

➡ Discounts are on offer throughout the year, especially during the summer months (May to September).

➡ Most hotels are child-friendly and of a very high standard.

➡ Dry hotels (no alcohol licence) are often a cheaper option.

Useful Websites

Lonely Planet Hotels (www.lonelyplanet.com/hotels) Lonely Planet's online booking service, with the lowdown on the best places to stay.

Visit Abu Dhabi (www.visitabudhabi.ae) The city's official tourism website gives useful information, including places to stay.

Abu Dhabi Bookings & City Guide (www.abudhabi.com) Covers a wide selection of capital hotels.

Dnata (www.dnatatravel.com) Local hotel listings.

Best Budget

Ibis Hotel Abu Dhabi Gate (www.ibis.com) One of the few modern budget hotels in Abu Dhabi, it offers excellent value for money, midway between town and the airport.

Aloft Abu Dhabi (www.aloftabudhabi.com) Adjoining the ADNEC Exhibition Centre, the loft-like rooms, rooftop pool and high-tech gadgetry make this a stylish business option.

Centro Yas Island (www.rotana.com) In the centre of the Yas hotel district, this contemporary choice has compact rooms for the budget conscious and attracts a younger crowd.

Al Jazeera Royal Hotel (www.aljaziraroyal.ae) With some of the cheapest rates in town, this friendly little hotel opposite the gold souq offers a feel for local life. No bar.

Best Midrange

Crowne Plaza Abu Dhabi (www.crowneplaza.com) A thoroughly amenable hotel, with generous rooms, grand views of the city, excellent service and a sociable experience.

Sheraton Abu Dhabi Hotel & Resort (www.sheratonabudhabihotel.com) A faded city centre icon in which to unwind in landscaped gardens or dip a toe in the hotel's private lagoon.

Viceroy Yas Abu Dhabi (www.viceroyhotelsandresorts.com) Appealing especially to race-goers, this dramatic hotel sits in pole position, straddling the Yas Marina Circuit.

Khalidiya Palace Rayhaan by Rotana (www.rotana.com) With a relaxed atmosphere, this dry hotel (no alcohol) appeals to families seeking a weekend getaway.

Which Part of Town?

Western Corniche Top-notch hotels are clustered at the end of the Corniche promising an exceptional experience in the region's best pleasure domes.

Al Markaziyah East & Al Zahiyah Good-value, midrange favourites are scattered within walking distance of the key downtown sights.

Islands Saadiyat is home to luxury beach resorts, Yas has activity-based hotels good for weekend breaks and Al Maryah promises new urban chic.

Khor al Maqta Offering great dining, Grand Mosque views and a beach by the *khor*, hotels here are neither city nor seaside and feel a tad raw.

Best Top End

Emirates Palace (www.emiratespalace.com) An overnight stay at this Abu Dhabi landmark offers a whole new dimension on an already class act.

Jumeirah at Etihad Towers (www.jumeirah.com) An exceptional hotel, occupying a landmark tower – one of five that rise from the end of the Corniche like polished organ pipes.

St Regis Abu Dhabi (www.stregisabudhabi.com) Strung between the top floors of the Nation Towers, the hotel's exclusive Abu Dhabi suite daringly inhabits a skybridge. Ordinary mortals stay in more grounded luxury.

Park Hyatt Abu Dhabi (abudhabi.park.hyatt.com) With a sandy beach surrounded by nature reserve and an infinity pool eye-to-eye with the open Gulf, this low-rise luxury hotel offers a perfect retreat.

Arriving in Abu Dhabi

☑ **Top Tip** For the best way to reach your accommodation, see p16.

Abu Dhabi International Airport

Airport Shuttle (A1 Bus; www.abudhabiairport.ae; one way Dh4; ⏱24hr) This air-conditioned airport shuttle leaves from the arrivals area of all terminals every 40 minutes. It stops at all legal bus stops along Hwy2, including the main bus station, and terminates at the City Terminal Check-In in Al Zahiyah (45 minutes).

Airport Taxi (www.abudhabiairport.ae; Abu Dhabi International Airport; metered fare from Dh25 plus Dh1.6/km) Metered taxis depart from all three terminals. The journey downtown takes about 45 minutes, depending on traffic. A luxury service is also available with multilingual male and female drivers and fares payable in multiple currencies.

From Dubai

Bus Modern air-conditioned buses leave Dubai's Al Ghubaiba Bus Station every 40 minutes (single/return Dh20/40) between 6am and 11pm. The trip takes about two hours and buses terminate at the **main bus terminal** (Sheikh Rashid

Smoking Regulations

New laws governing smoking came into effect in January 2015 throughout the UAE. The key facts are as follows:

➡ No smoking in public places.

➡ *Sheesha* smoking is prohibited under the age of 18.

➡ Smoking is still permitted in designated hotel rooms and some bars and nightclubs.

➡ There are fines for throwing cigarette butts into the street and for smoking in non-smoking areas.

bin Saeed St (cnr 4th & 11th Sts), near Al Wahda Mall) in Al Wahdah.

Car The drive on well-maintained, signposted highways takes about two hours.

Long Distance Taxis An intercity service plying routes from Dubai and other destinations such as Al Ain is run by **Al Ghazal** (☑02-550 2160; www.alghazalcar-rental. com). They arrive and depart near the main bus terminal.

Getting Around

Bicycle
☑ **Best for**...exercise

➡ A great way to appreciate the modern skyline of Abu Dhabi's western shore is to cycle along a dedicated bike path on the Corniche.

➡ Bicycles (men's, women's and children's) are available for rent at four stations along the road, with the most reliably manned at the far western end of the road, near the Hiltonia Beach Club.

Ojra Cards & Bus Passes
Abu Dhabi Bus Services offers the following discounts through their Ojra bus pass. Ojra cards can be purchased from the office at the **Main Bus Terminal** (Sheikh Rashid bin Saeed St, cnr 4th & 11th Sts, near Al Wahda Mall) on Al Murror Rd.

Weekly Bus Pass Dh30

Monthly Bus Pass Dh80

Senior Citizens (over 60) Free

Bus
☑ **Best for**...on a budget

Abu Dhabi Bus Services (☑800 55 555; dot.abudhabi. ae; within Abu Dhabi Dh2) Abu Dhabi has a good public transport system with regular buses around the city. It also links to the suburbs and provides intercity links. Bus routes are available on the website. The standard fare is payable upon boarding the bus.

Shuttle
☑ **Best for**...Yas Island

Yas Express (☑02-496 8110; www.yasisland. ae; ⏰9am-9pm) This complimentary bus service connects all the major attractions on Yas Island at regular intervals throughout the day. A more limited night route

operates until 2am. There is also a shuttle between Yas Island and Saadiyat Island between 10am and 8pm. Route maps are available on the website.

Taxi
☑ **Best for**...convenience

Abu Dhabi Taxi (☑600-535 353; www.transad.ae) This government-monitored service runs metered taxis and operates a women's cab service.

Tour Bus
☑ **Best for**...sightseeing

➡ For an informative introduction to the city, the hop-on hop-off service by **Big Bus** (☑02-449 0026; www.bigbustours.com; 24hr adult/child Dh200/100, 48hr adult/child Dh260/130; ⏰9am-7pm) is hard to beat. The route lasts 90 minutes and passes all the major sights, including Sheikh Zayed Grand Mosque, the Corniche, the Heritage Village and Emirates Palace Hotel.

➡ Tickets, which include free headphones, are available online and from hotels and kiosks next to the Big Bus stops.

Essential Information

Electricity

220V/50Hz

➡ Voltage is 220V AC; British-style three-pin wall sockets are standard.

➡ Adaptors are inexpensive and available at supermarkets.

Emergency

Ambulance (☏999)

Fire Department (☏997)

Police (☏999)

Medical Services

Sheikh Khalifa Medical City (☏02-610 2000; www.skmc.ae; Al Bateen St) One of many well-equipped hospitals in the city with 24-hour emergency services. For locations of 24-hour pharmacies, call ☏777 929.

Money

☑ **Top Tip** Check if rates include the mandatory 10% service charge and 6% tourism fee.

ATMs

Many credit and debit cards can be used for withdrawing money from ATMs. There is usually a charge (around 1.5% to 2%) on ATM cash withdrawals abroad.

Changing Money

There are 21 branches of **UAE Exchange** (☏02-644 1190; www.uaeexchange.com) in Abu Dhabi, including in each of the malls, offering better rates than banks.

Credit Cards

Visa, MasterCard and American Express are widely accepted at shops, hotels and restaurants throughout Dubai and Abu Dhabi, and debit cards are accepted at bigger retail outlets.

Tipping

A few extra dirhams in change is welcomed by waiters in the cheaper restaurants. In hotel restaurants, service charges are included.

Opening Hours

☑ **Top Tip** Note that hours are limited during Ramadan.

The United Arab Emirates (UAE) weekend is on Friday and Saturday.

Banks 8am to 1pm (some until 3pm) Sunday to Thursday, 8am to noon Saturday

Restaurants noon to 3pm and 7.30pm to midnight

Shopping malls 10am to 10pm Sunday to Wednesday, 10am to midnight Thursday to Saturday

Souqs & markets 9am to 1pm and 4pm to 9pm Saturday to Thursday, 4pm to 9pm Friday

Public Holidays

☑ **Top Tip** Many restaurants and bars close during Ramadan; drinking and entertainment is restricted.

Public holidays include 1st January and UAE National Day on 2nd and 3rd December. Religious holidays, determined by the lunar calendar, are announced in the papers (www.thenational.ae).

Hejira Islamic New Year

Eid al Fitr Marks the end of Ramadan fasting and is a three-day celebration.

Eid al Adha A four-day celebration following the main pilgrimage to Mecca, the hajj.

Ramadan Month of fasting during daylight hours.

Prophet's Birthday Varies annually according to the Islamic (lunar) calendar.

Safe Travel

☑ **Top Tip** Dressing in a culturally appropriate way (shoulders and knees covered) avoids offending local sensibilities and attracting unwanted attention.

Crime Abu Dhabi is a very safe city to travel around during the day or night.

Women Can safely take taxis on their own but they may encounter unwanted attention, especially if walking alone.

Drugs The UAE has zero tolerance towards illegal drugs. Having illegal substances in your bloodstream counts as possession.

Traffic The UAE has a poor record when it comes to traffic-related accidents. If you're involved in an accident, don't move the car until the police arrive.

Telephone

☑ **Top Tip** Local calls (within the same area code) are free.

➜ UAE country code (☎0971)

➜ Local directory services (☎181)

➜ International directory assistance (☎151)

➜ Abu Dhabi area code (☎02)

➜ Dubai area code (☎04)

➜ The UAE's mobile phone network uses the GSM 900 MHz and 1800 MHz standard. Mobile numbers begin with either ☎050 (Etisalat) or ☎055 (Du). If your phone is unlocked, consider buying a prepaid SIM card, available at the airport and citywide stores.

➜ 3G is widely available.

Islamic Holidays

ISLAMIC YEAR	HEJIRA	PROPHET'S BIRTHDAY	RAMADAN	EID AL FITR	EID AL ADHA
1436 (2015)	25 Oct	24 Dec	18 Jun	17 Jul	23 Sep
1437 (2016)	3 Oct	12 Dec	7 Jun	7 Jul	13 Sep
1438 (2017)	22 Sep	1 Dec	27 May	26 Jun	2 Sep

Tourist Information

☑ **Top Tip** Touchscreen kiosks provide information for travellers at all key attractions, hotels and resorts.

Abu Dhabi Tourism Authority (ADTA; ☑ toll free 800 555; www. visitabudhabi.ae) Maintains information desks in the airport arrivals hall and in Khalifa Park (☑ 02-444 0444, toll free 800 555; www. tcaabudhabi.ae; Khalifa Park; ⊙ 8am-2pm Sun-Thu), Ferrari World (☑ 02-496 8000; www. ferrariworldabudhabi.com; Yas Island; adult/child under 1.3m Dh250/205, premium admission Dh450/365; ⊙ 11am-8pm, seasonal variations) and Souq Central Market (☑ 02-810 7810; www.central-market.ae/souk; Khalifa St; ⊙ 10am-10pm Sun-Thu, to 11pm Fri & Sat).

Travellers with Disabilities

☑ **Top Tip** Some ramps are very steep. Double-check before booking at hotels.

➡ The big sights, such as Sheikh Zayed Grand Mosque, the Emirates Palace, Yas Island and Masdar City, all have facilities for those in wheelchairs; all midrange and five-star hotels have lifts (elevators).

➡ There is a special check-in gate for travellers with special needs and a meet-and-assist service at Abu Dhabi International Airport.

Visas

➡ Free visas valid for 30 days are available on arrival by air and at border crossings for 45 nationalities including most Western nationals.

➡ Check the following website for further information: www.abudhabi airport.ae.

Language

MSA (Modern Standard Arabic) –
the official lingua franca of the Arab
world – and the everyday spoken
version are quite different. The Arabic
variety spoken in Dubai (and provided
in this chapter) is known as Gulf Arabic.

Note that *gh* is a throaty sound
(like the French 'r'), *r* is rolled, *dh* is
pronounced as the 'th' in 'that', *th* as in
'thin', *ch* as in 'cheat' and *kh* as the 'ch'
in the Scottish *loch*. The apostrophe
(') indicates the glottal stop (like the
pause in the middle of 'uh-oh'). Bearing
these few points in mind and reading
our pronunciation guides as if they
were English, you'll be understood.
The stressed syllables are indicated
with italics. The markers (m) and (f)
indicate masculine and feminine word
forms respectively.

To enhance your trip with a phrase-
book, visit **lonelyplanet.com**.

Basics

Hello.
اهلا و سهلا. *ah*·lan was *ah*·lan

Goodbye.
مع السلامة. ma'·sa·*laa*·ma

Yes./No.
نعم.لا. na·'am/la

Please.
من فضلك. min *fad*·lak (m)
من فضلك. min *fad*·lik (f)

Thank you.
شكران. *shuk*·ran

Excuse me.
اسمح لي. is·*mah* lee (m)
اسمحي لي. is·mah·*ee* lee (f)

Sorry.
مع الاسف. ma' al·*as*·af

Do you speak English?
تتكلم/تتكلمي tit·*kal*·am/tit·*ka*·la·mee
انجليزية؟ in·glee·*zee*·ya (m/f)

I don't understand.
مو فاهم. moo *faa*·him

Eating & Drinking

I'd like (the) ..., please.
عطني/عطيني *a*·ti·nee/*a*·*tee*·nee
الـ ... من فضلك. il ... min *fad*·lak (m/f)

bill	قائمة	*kaa*·'i·ma
drink list	قائمة المشروبات	*kaa*·'i·mat il·mash·roo·*baat*
menu	قائمة الطعام	*kaa*·'i·mat i·ta·*'aam*
that dish	الطبق هاذاك	i·*tab*·ak *haa*·dhaa·ka

What would you recommend?
اش تنصح؟ aash *tan*·sah (m)
اش تنصحي؟ aash *tan*·sa·hee (f)

Do you have vegetarian food?
عندك طعم *an*·dak ta·*'am*
نباتي؟ na·*baa*·tee

Shopping

I'm looking for ...
مدور على ... moo·*daw*·ir ·*a*·la ... (m)
مدورة على ... moo·*daw*·i·ra ·*a*·la ... (f)

Can I look at it?
ممكن اشوف؟ *mum*·kin a·*shoof*

How much is it?
بكم؟ bi·*kam*

That's too expensive.
غالي جدا. ghaa·lee jid·an

What's your lowest price?
اش السعر الاخر؟ aash i·si'r il·aa·khir

Do you have any others?
عندك اخرين؟ 'and·ak ukh·reen (m)
عندك اخرين؟ 'and·ik ukh·reen (f)

Emergencies

Help!
مساعد! moo·saa·'id (m)
مساعدة! moo·saa·'id·a (f)

Call a doctor!
تصل/تصلي ti·sil/ti·si·lee
على طبيب! 'a·la ta·beeb (m/f)

Call the police!
تصل/تصلي ti·sil/ti·si·lee
على الشرطة! 'a·la i·shur·ta (m/f)

I'm lost.
انا ضعت. a·na duht

I'm sick.
انا مريض. a·na ma·reed (m)
انا مريضة. a·na ma·ree·da (f)

Where are the toilets?
وين المرحاض؟ wayn il·mir·haad

Time & Numbers

What time is it?/At what time?
الساعة كم؟ i·saa·a' kam

It's/At (two) o'clock.
الساعة (ثنتين). i·saa·a' (thin·tayn)

yesterday ...	البارح ...	il·baa·rih ...
tomorrow ...	باكر ...	baa·chir ...
morning	صباح	sa·baah
afternoon	بعد الظهر	ba'd a·thuhr
evening	مساء	mi·saa

1	١	واحد	waa·hid
2	٢	اثنين	ith·nayn
3	٣	ثلاثة	tha·laa·tha
4	٤	اربع	ar·ba'
5	٥	خمسة	kham·sa
6	٦	ستة	si·ta
7	٧	سبعة	sa·ba'
8	٨	ثمانية	tha·maan·ya
9	٩	تسعة	tis·a'
10	١٠	عشرة	'ash·ar·a
100	١٠٠	مية	mee·ya
1000	١٠٠٠	الف	alf

Transport & Directions

Where's the ...?
من وين ...؟ min wayn ...

What's the address?
ما العنوان؟ ma il·'un·waan

Can you show me (on the map)?
لو سمحت law sa·maht
وريني wa·ree·nee
(علخريطة)؟ ('al·kha·ree·ta)

How far is it?
كم بعيد؟ kam ba·'eed

Please take me to (this address).
من فضلك خذني min fad·lak khudh·nee
(علعنوان هاذا). ('al·'un·waan haa·dha)

Please stop here.
لو سمحت law sa·maht
وقف هنا. wa·gif hi·na

What time's the bus?
الساعة كم a·saa·a' kam
الباص؟ il·baas

What station/stop is this?
ما هي maa hee·ya
المحطة هاذي؟ il·ma·ha·ta haa·dhee

Behind the Scenes

Send Us Your Feedback

We love to hear from travellers – your comments help make our books better. We read every word, and we guarantee that your feedback goes straight to the authors. Visit **lonelyplanet.com/contact** to submit your updates and suggestions.

Note: We may edit, reproduce and incorporate your comments in Lonely Planet products such as guidebooks, websites and digital products, so let us know if you don't want your comments reproduced or your name acknowledged. For a copy of our privacy policy visit lonelyplanet.com/privacy.

Jenny's Thanks

Abu Dhabi is a fast-changing city, impossible to capture without insightful input from residents. Thanks are due, therefore, to all our regional friends who have helped with this project. To my beloved husband, Sam Owen, I reserve unqualified thanks for going beyond the call of duty during research and write-up.

Acknowledgments

Cover photograph: Sheikh Zayed Grand Mosque, Abu Dhabi; Jon Hicks/Corbis.

This Book

This 1st edition of Lonely Planet's *Pocket Abu Dhabi* guidebook was researched and written by Jenny Walker. This guidebook was produced by the following:

Destination Editor Helen Elfer **Product Editors** Elin Berglund, Kate Kiely **Regional Senior Cartographer** David Kemp **Book Designer** Virginia Moreno **Assisting Editors** Gabrielle Innes, Christopher Pitts **Cover Researcher** Naomi Parker **Thanks to** Claire Naylor, Karyn Noble, Martine Power

Index

See also separate subindexes for:

Eating p156

Drinking p157

Entertainment p157

Shopping p157

Sights 000

Map Pages **000**

Our Writer

Jenny Walker

Jenny Walker's first involvement with Arabia was as a student, collecting butterflies for her father's book in Saudi Arabia. She went on to write a dissertation on Doughty and Lawrence (Stirling University) and a MPhil thesis on the Arabic Orient in British Literature (Oxford University). Current PhD studies (Nottingham Trent University) focus on Arabian deserts in contemporary literature. A member of the British Guild of Travel Writers and the Outdoor Writers and Photographers Guild, she has written extensively on the Middle East and lived in Oman for the past 16 years. With her husband, Wing Commander (retired) Sam Owen, she co-authored *Off-Road in the Sultanate of Oman*. Jenny has travelled in over 110 countries and is Associate Dean of an engineering college in Muscat.

Published by Lonely Planet Publications Pty Ltd
ABN 36 005 607 983
1st edition – Sep 2015
ISBN 978 1 74360 515 8
© Lonely Planet 2015   Photographs © as indicated 2015
10 9 8 7 6 5 4 3 2 1
Printed in China